MAC
BALDRIGE

Kim—
To a real
survivor!

MAC
BALDRIGE

THE COWBOY IN
RONALD REAGAN'S CABINET

Chris

CHRIS BLACK AND
B. JAY COOPER

B. Jay

Foreword by
President George H. W. Bush

LYONS PRESS
Guilford, Connecticut

Published by Lyons Press
An imprint of Rowman & Littlefield

Distributed by NATIONAL BOOK NETWORK

British Library Cataloguing in Publication Information Available

Library of Congress Cataloging-in-Publication Data
Black, Christine M., author.
  Mac Baldrige : the cowboy in Ronald Reagan's cabinet / Chris Black and B. Jay Cooper ; with a foreword by President George H. W. Bush.
  pages cm
  ISBN 978-1-4930-1799-7 (cloth : alk. paper) — ISBN 978-1-4930-1800-0 (electronic)
  1. Baldrige, Malcolm, 1922–1987. 2. Cabinet officers—United States—Biography. 3. United States. Department of Commerce—Officials and employees—Biography. 4. United States—Politics and government—1981–1989. I. Cooper, B. Jay. II. Title. III. Title: Cowboy in Ronald Reagan's cabinet.
  E840.8.B317B53 2015
  352.2'93092—dc23
  [B]

                                                    2015024731

∞™ The paper used in this publication meets the minimum requirements of American National Standard for Information Sciences—Permanence of Paper for Printed Library Materials, ANSI/NISO Z39.48-1992.

Printed in the United States of America

CONTENTS

FOREWORD

President George H. W. Bush

MAC BALDRIGE WAS A CLOSE, GOOD, AND STRONG FRIEND, a friend for life. He acted as a key political advisor, but he was first and foremost my friend.

In 1980 I asked Mac to be my campaign chairman in Connecticut, a state that emerged in that presidential election as a key state during the early primary season. While I won the Iowa caucus in an upset, then-governor Ronald Reagan beat me soundly in New Hampshire, giving him a boost that threatened to leave the rest of us in the dust. The Connecticut primary took place in March, and the conventional wisdom said that if I lost to Governor Reagan there, one of my home states, then my candidacy was over.

So I went to Connecticut and spent a full week there campaigning as if I were running for governor, driving around the state with Mac in a Winnebago driven by a young Tom Collamore, who later served with distinction with Mac at the Commerce Department and with me at the White House. Mac and I spent many hours in that Winnebago driving from New Haven where we both went to college to the narrow back roads of Litchfield County to the tiny towns near New York in Fairfield County and down the seacoast to New London and back up to the Rhode Island border. We plotted campaign strategy, told stories, shared jokes, and laughed a lot. We carried the state. That kept my campaign alive and moved my political fortunes forward, as I eventually served as President Reagan's vice president, and later as president.

Mac became the U.S. Secretary of Commerce at my urging. He was among the best who ever held that job. Why? Mac came to the position wanting nothing from it. He only wanted to give back and to serve his country, again. He served his country well during World War II in Asia, and he served it equally well when President Reagan named him to his cabinet.

He performed breakthrough work on U.S.-China trade; helped pass the Export Trading Company Act; tried to reorganize the government's trade functions; and got the nation's industries focused on productivity and competitiveness, which led to a much-sought-after award being named for him, the Malcolm Baldrige National Quality Award. He provided candid, informed, and thoughtful counsel to President Reagan on every issue from trade to taxes. Mac's service was solid, and he exerted major influence on our country's progress and policies.

He excelled at his cabinet job in part because he had been so successful in the private sector, running Scovill, Inc. He brought practical, real-life experience to the table. He thought first of the people we served, developing opportunities for job creation, just as he always thought first about his employees at Scovill when he was in Waterbury, Connecticut. He never looked for the next step—to run for office or to move around in the cabinet ranks. As I liked to think, we want folks, like Mac, who will take "a step down" to serve in the government because they are focused on the job, not on personal gain.

President Reagan was shot and seriously wounded less than three months after taking office in 1981. Many in the administration rushed to the Situation Room at the White House, wanting to be part of the "action." Mac didn't go to the Sit Room. He knew I was flying back from Texas. Instead of making a big public scene, he quietly called my wife, Barbara, to say that if I needed anything, he was there. He did not have to make that call. I always knew Mac had my back.

For several years Mac and his wife, Midge, were our guests on Memorial Day weekend in Kennebunkport, usually with Sen. Alan Simpson and his wife, Ann. I used to speak at the Kennebunkport Memorial Day parade about the special meaning of the holiday for me. One year, I asked Mac to speak, and he delivered a moving account of the conflicts of war, the agony of taking a life, and the possibility of reconciliation and forgiveness. As always, Mac used very few words to tell his story. But he said so much. I had never heard him speak in public about his wartime experiences, and it is a testimony to the power of our friendship that he shared those stories then.

Mac, sticking to his cowboy ethic, did not speak often or long at cabinet meetings, but when he did, people listened. And I must admit, sometimes we passed notes back and forth to each other for our own amusement. Usually, those notes were the latest jokes we each enjoyed!

He had a zest for life, a deep and abiding love for his family. Megan and Molly revered him. Midge adored him. And he gave that back and more to them.

I remember one evening in the early 1980s. The Commerce Department softball team (called "The Big

Mac Attack") played the team from my Office of the Vice President. My phone at the Vice President's Residence rang, and it was Mac. I thought, oh no, there must be an international trade problem or some emergency. But there was no crisis. Mac called from the sidelines at the softball game. He said to me, "My team is kicking your team's ass out here and you better get over here to cheer your people on!"

In the mid-1980s, when I was thinking of running for president in 1988, I held frequent and quiet strategy discussions with a very small circle of my most trusted friends and advisors. That early group included Mac Baldrige.

When Mac died in the roping accident in California, I had just returned from fishing at Kennebunkport. His death was a deep shock and, for me, a grievous loss. I lowered the American flag at Walker's Point in Mac's honor. Mac, an honest and good man, was indeed the noblest work of God. I not only lost a great friend that day, I lost someone who was like my brother.

INTRODUCTION

Megan and Molly Baldrige

OUR FATHER, MAC BALDRIGE, EXCELLED AT MANY THINGS: he was a skilled team roper, an astute businessman, a distinguished U.S. Commerce Secretary. But most importantly, he was a wonderful father to us, his two daughters. While Mac often traveled for work or for rodeos, he always reserved time for his girls when he returned, focusing on each of us so that we felt much loved. While we were growing up, he turned down many work-related invitations to be home for family breakfasts and suppers. We often rode horses with him. He used those rides to dispense a continuous font of cowboy wisdom and logic drawn from his experiences as a cowboy and as a soldier in Japan. On horseback, we were effectively a captive audience for his hard-earned wisdom. As teenagers we felt we heard the same advice over and over, but now we try to remember every wise word. We were grateful when our friends visited, so that

Mac had a wider audience, and to this day, they quote his words with appreciation.

When we were young, Megan remembers Mac returning home after a long business trip abroad and heading to the school playground to see her. "Dads didn't usually visit their children on the playground, but Mac did, and he was welcomed by other children who enjoyed his questions to them about their homework. On this particular day, he talked to me for a few minutes, then turned to chat with Raymond, a struggling math student, and asked him about our recent math quiz. I was miffed that Mac was less interested in my quiz than he was in my classmate's effort, but Mac later explained that he had felt Raymond needed some extra attention, whereas he trusted that I was doing just fine.

"When I was twenty-one and had gotten my first post-college job working as a part-time reporter for a local Connecticut newspaper, Mac was absolutely delighted that I had a job but also openly pleased that my new boss went out of his way to express his disdain for me. My boss's lack of confidence in me, and my father's certain faith in me, motivated me to work extra hard—to prove myself. Mac would chortle at my editor's rude comments, saying, 'You don't know how lucky you are to have Chuck as your first boss; you couldn't ask for a better boss; every other boss you have is going to be a relief.' After work, he loved to help me construct the critically important lede for future stories. His love of good writing and interest in human nature made him a good teacher and a good writer."

Molly remembers Mac's kindness and understanding that eased her through the awkward teenage years. "I was on my way to a boy-girl party in seventh grade, scared, feeling unattractive and shy. Dad understood how I felt, and he sat me down to offer a more global perspective. He said, 'Molly, everyone at the party will be feeling the same way you do.

Your job is to find the most unpopular and miserable person at the party, go talk to him, draw him out, make him feel good about himself, give him some confidence. When you do that, you'll be doing a kindness for him, but beyond that, you'll stop thinking about yourself, and that's what is really important.' Molly also used, and passed along to her own children, Mac's excellent advice about how to start the new school year (or any new undertaking). He always said, 'Hit it hard right from the beginning. How you start is how you'll be remembered by the teacher, and if you have to slack off sometime later on, you'll have the benefit of the doubt. But if you start off slow, it's hard to ever catch up, especially in the eyes of the teacher.'"

Mac was cool in everything he did, in all the different senses of the word. While we thought then that he lectured us way too much, in reality, he showed us more than told us, he was never inane, he rarely got angry, he was funny and silly but never undignified, and he was a great model of how a person could be hard-working, ethical, straight, and honest, all while being cool, even in the eyes of tough teenage critics. For example, when we were eight and ten years old, a new musical phenomenon called the Beatles was scheduled to perform on TV on a Sunday night. This was past our school night bedtime, but Mac understood the importance of this event to our cultural development and insisted that we stay up to see them. Later, when *A Hard Day's Night,* the first feature film starring our beloved Beatles, played in the downtown Waterbury, Connecticut, movie theater, Mac waited in a long line on a weekday morning to get matinee tickets for all of us to see the movie. He was the only adult, and certainly the only person in a business suit, waiting happily among throngs of loud teenagers. Instead of being embarrassed by his business associates driving by and seeing him in this situation, he was proud of having a foot in this world, too.

Mac has been much missed since his death, at the prime of his life in 1987. Two of his seven grandchildren met their grandfather as infants; all the grandchildren have had to rely on our treasury of stories to know a little of the grandfather whom they would have thoroughly enjoyed. Recently, as our children all passed the twenty-one-year-old threshold, we wanted them to know more about what made Mac a successful leader in Washington so that they might benefit from his story. We realized that the time was right to ask Mac's press secretary and friend, B. Jay Cooper, if he would write a book describing Mac's years in Washington. B. Jay agreed, as long as he could share the project with his wife, former *Boston Globe* and CNN reporter Chris Black, who had written a number of books. They immediately went to work interviewing dozens of former colleagues to reconstruct Mac's life in Washington.

We dedicate this book to Mac's grandchildren: Malcolm, Fonda, Mac, Jack, Diego, Parry, and Bry. We wish that you could have known this soft-spoken, strong, kind man. Short of that, we hope that you, and others, will enjoy reading about some of the life and accomplishments of our beloved father.

1

=

MAC THE MAN

FROM THE START, MAC BALDRIGE STOOD OUT IN
Washington. The hardened news reporters who covered politics and government in Washington were charmed by the
very idea of a lean, laconic, card-carrying member of the
Professional Rodeo Cowboys Association (PRCA) serving in
President Ronald Reagan's cabinet. Presidents typically named
a bland businessman to head up the Commerce Department,
often someone who raised a lot of money for the president's
political campaign. The position was considered a second-
or third-tier cabinet post. But Mac was different: he rode
horses and roped steers. He maintained his qualifications for
membership in the PRCA by winning money in team roping
competitions each year. Team roping involves two cowboys:
a "header" and a "heeler." Mac was always the "heeler" who
deftly whipped his lasso around the steer's hind legs after his
partner roped the head, all in six to nine seconds. To keep

in practice, he routinely lassoed his secretary and other staff members in his cavernous Commerce Department office during impromptu demonstrations for visitors, including foreign dignitaries and reporters. Nearly every newspaper and magazine profile about him dutifully recorded his status in the cowboy world. In July 1981, a *New York Times* article carried the headline "Commerce Chief: Malcolm Baldrige; The Quiet Cowboy in Mr. Reagan's Posse." There were plenty of other cowboy headlines: "Cabinet's Cowboy Will Keep Tight Rein on Business," "Yankee Executive at Home on Range," "A Cowboy from Connecticut," "Rough Riding Ahead for Mac Baldrige."

Mac had little patience with the cowboy fixation. The *Wall Street Journal* quoted him as saying, "Yahoo, yippee, cowboy comes to Wall Street. It makes me Yuk." Yet few reporters could resist the story line and often used cowboy analogies in any story involving Mac; policy debates were always "wrangles." In those days, cabinet secretaries and senior White House advisers were mostly older white men. There might be one black man and one woman in the mix, but generally presidents picked people who looked like them to staff their government. The cowboy is a quintessential American icon, far from the typical image of the staid senior government official. It gave Mac special status right away.

Ronald Reagan did not know Mac very well when he asked him to serve in his cabinet. Mac had supported George H. W. Bush, Reagan's primary challenger for the 1980 Republican presidential nomination. Bush was a longtime Baldrige friend, a former member of Congress, U.S. envoy to China, Central Intelligence Agency (CIA) director, and Republican National Committee chairman. After a vigorous campaign, Reagan chose Bush as his running mate, a gesture that brought together warring elements of the party. The Republican National Convention in Detroit ratified the decision. Reagan went on to defeat incumbent President Jimmy Carter to win the presidency.

In fact, Mac was George Bush's pick, the only Bush man in the Reagan cabinet. Protocol required that the president-elect notify the lucky choice himself, so Reagan called the Baldrige farm in Woodbury, Connecticut, the day after Thanksgiving in 1980, just weeks after election day. Mac's wife, Midge, answered the telephone. The voice may have been vaguely familiar, but she did not realize who was calling when she first answered the phone.

When the caller asked for Mac, she politely explained that Mac would be unavailable for the next three hours, because he was out riding and roping with friends. According to news accounts, Reagan grinned, slapped his knee, and declared, "That's my kind of man!" When the caller identified himself, Midge later told an Associated Press reporter, "I was astonished. I said, 'You must be joking.'"

He was not. Their lives were about to change. With a touch of resignation, Midge said she would have to put aside her blue jeans and her country life and buy some high heels and nice clothes to go to Washington, D.C., as the spouse of a cabinet official. She ended up having a grand time, as did Mac. As much as she liked her life in rural Woodbury, she enjoyed the intellectual stimulation and excitement of being in the center of power in Washington.

The future secretary's name at birth was Howard Malcolm Baldrige Jr. Years before his appointment to the cabinet, Mac legally changed his name, dropping the Howard in favor of the simpler Malcolm Baldrige. At the time Reagan appointed him, Mac was the fifty-eight-year-old board chairman and chief executive officer of Scovill, Inc., a onetime brass works in the old mill city of Waterbury, Connecticut, about twelve miles from Woodbury.

By any measurement, Mac was a success. Scovill was founded as a brass mill in 1802. For generations, the manufacturing company made ammunition and the buttons worn on military uniforms (for the first time in the War of 1812), as well as other everyday items made from brass. As plastics replaced brass in the manufacture of many products from buttons to plumbing fixtures, the original factory languished. In the 1960s and 1970s, Mac sold Scovill's brass divisions, saved the pensions of longtime employees, and diversified Scovill's holdings into a variety of successful businesses with plants throughout the world. By the time he left the company, Scovill was the world's largest manufacturer of tire valves, and a major manufacturer of items ranging from snap fasteners and zippers to automobile dashboards, lipstick cases, and small household appliances. The company divisions included two of the nation's best-known brands, Hamilton Beach and Yale Locks, one of the nation's oldest lock companies. Sales reached nearly $1 billion a year by 1980.

Mac was not only a business success. He had been happily married for nearly thirty years to the inestimable Midge, and they had raised two daughters, Megan and Molly, who had graduated from college and were establishing their own careers. He was prosperous, well regarded by his peers, active in his community, a highly respected Republican Party fund-raiser and leader in Connecticut, and he was eager to serve his country.

While Mac never won election to public office, politics had always been part of his life. His father, Howard Malcolm Baldrige Sr., served in the state legislature in Nebraska; won election as a delegate to the Republican Presidential Nominating Conventions in the 1920s, a time when convention delegates actually selected the party nominees for the highest offices in the land; and then won a seat in the U.S. House in 1930, when Mac was eight years old. He lost his seat after a single term in the 1932 Franklin D. Roosevelt land-slide, when Roosevelt crushed President Herbert Hoover and swept ninety new Democrats into the U.S. House in the first years of the Great Depression.

His daughters remember that Mac revered his father as well as his father's brother, Thomas J. Baldrige, a lawyer, for-mer Pennsylvania attorney general, and longtime judge from Hollidaysburg, Pennsylvania. The senior Baldriges were men of integrity, dignity, and accomplishment with a strong sense of public service, and each served as a powerfully influential role model for the young Mac. His father not only ran for public office but also enlisted and served in the military dur-ing both world wars. Mac came of age during World War II, and he, too, enlisted in the army immediately upon gradua-tion from Yale in 1944. He served in the 27th Infantry Division in the Pacific Theater for the final year of the war and the beginning of the Occupation of Japan.

Mac was born in Omaha in 1922. Two siblings, Robert Connell (Bob) and Letitia (Tish), followed two and four years later. Bob graduated from Yale in the class of 1945W, a special wartime class, and he joined his older brother and their father in the army in World War II. He earned a Bronze Star. After the war, he became a textile executive in New York. He grew tired of the persistent misspelling of his last name and decided to add back the second *d* that had been dropped many generations earlier and legally changed his name to "Baldridge." Mac and Tish chose not to do so, so three siblings had two different spellings of their last name. After Vassar, Tish was social secretary to Evangeline Bruce, wife of the French ambassador, and then to Clare Boothe Luce, the U.S. ambassador to Italy. She became the first female executive at Tiffany's, heading the public rela-tions department, before working as First Lady Jacqueline Kennedy's social secretary in the White House. After her

White House days, she ran her own public relations firm and wrote many etiquette books, beginning with an update of Amy Vanderbilt's book on manners.

When Mac was born, Nebraska had only been a state for fifty-five years. The Nebraska of his youth was largely rural grain fields and grazing lands. The state had been developed by adventurous settlers who received 160 acres of land from the government in return for living on and working the land under the terms of the Homestead Act of 1862. That Civil War–era law was intended to give immigrants, freed slaves, and poor whites from the South the opportunity to become independent landowners and farmers, and to begin to develop the vast acreage that sprawled west of the Mississippi River. Nebraska suffered like the rest of the region from the devastating afflictions of a prolonged drought and the Great Depression in the 1930s. The drought and dust farms wiped out an estimated one hundred million acres of topsoil and farmland in the Dust Bowl.

While Mac grew up in comfortable circumstances as the son of a lawyer, he was aware of the suffering that was so pronounced and widespread at the time. His father's law practice was affected by the Depression. Even professionals struggled for paying customers in those dark years. When Mac Baldrige Sr. sent his first-born East to attend the Hotchkiss School, a preparatory school in Connecticut, he told young Mac he needed to earn some scholarship money if he wanted to go to college. Mac arrived at Hotchkiss wearing a green tweed suit with a belt in the back. His classmates teased him mercilessly for his "hick" attire. He never forgot the humiliation. Midge told a reporter years later that the experience made him vow that no one would ever make him feel that badly again. Mac overcame his difficult arrival from Nebraska at Hotchkiss and emerged as a leader of his class. He won a full scholarship to Yale and earned extra money selling suit-pressing contracts to students. For the rest of his life, he dressed carefully and appropriately.

According to the Pro Rodeo Hall of Fame, Mac was a confirmed cowboy by the age of seven. He idolized the hard-working, sunburnt warriors of the range and picked up their characteristic mannerisms. (He looked so much like a classic cowboy that Philip Morris & Company, then the manufacturer of the Marlboro cigarette, once approached him to model as the Marlboro man, the rugged and tough cowboy who gave the cigarettes their macho image in the company's advertising. Mac was a two-pack-a-day smoker for most of his life, like many men of his era. He declined the offer.)

By the age of twenty he had spent six summers working as a ranch hand, including a stint on a pig farm, for a dollar a day and room and board. It was a grueling job of twelve-hour days on the hay wagon six or seven days a week. He loved it, and he loved his fellow ranch hands. He acquired a great respect for the quiet stoicism, the independence and resilience of the cowboy. The experience gave him a measure of toughness not typically seen in a business executive.

Lionel Olmer, who served as Under Secretary of Commerce for International Trade under Mac, remembered Mac participated in a team roping contest in Aldie, Virginia, in 1984 with a frequent partner, Ken Schiffer, a Wyoming cowboy who worked as an FBI agent in the Washington office. He suddenly heard a shout of pain from the ring. Mac was wearing riding gloves, but his fingers got caught in his dally (the turns of rope around the saddle horn that fixes the lasso to the saddle once the roper catches the steer). He lost the tip of his right index finger and fractured the middle finger. He and Ken kept roping and won the contest and $100 prize money, which he split with Ken. Then his Commerce Department driver, Wesley "Wes" Goad, raced him to the nearest hospital in Leesburg at ninety miles per hour with lights flashing. A second car with his fingertip, safely nestled in a Pepsi cup full of ice, followed close behind. The next week he complained to reporters that he lost money on the deal. The hospital bill was $400. He remained an enthusiastic and expert roper throughout his life.

His daughters often accompanied him to practice sessions and competitions after work and on weekends when they were growing up in Connecticut. He proudly wore the large metal trophy belt buckles presented to victors with his bespoke double-breasted pin-striped suits made by Carmine Fabrizio of Madison Avenue. Fabrizio told a reporter that Mac upgraded the quality of his suits to the top "Cadillac" class when he went to Washington. The boy who was teased for his green tweed jacket was always impeccably turned out in his conservative handmade suits with white pocket squares.

Several times, Mac told a story to reporters that he believed demonstrated the biggest differences between the cowboy ethic and the rest of the world. When he was CEO of Scovill, Mac went to Colorado to compete in a rodeo with an old friend who was riding the circuit but not experiencing much luck. In fact, his friend had not won any prize money in two months. His wife and children, whom he supported, waited at home for him. This friend gave him a lift to Denver, and at the end of a long day, he suggested that Mac prepare their dinner. Mac found a couple of bottles of soda, a loaf of bread, and a jar of peanut butter in the cowboy's camper. His friend had been living on those meager stores for days, but he never complained. He just vowed to do better in the next competition and earn some prize money. Mac deeply admired the self-reliance of the cowboy way of life and delighted in the idea that a performance determined if you were going to eat steak or peanut butter for supper. When Mac returned to Connecticut, he said that a vice president at Scovill complained to him about the placement of his office. Mac gave the executive's complaint short shrift.

His younger sister, Tish, once told a reporter that her brother was a paradox, a mix of conflicting strains and qualities. He absorbed the ethos of his generation that had survived the Depression, fought in World War II, and then participated in building the postwar prosperity that made the United States the preeminent economic power in the world. The war united the generations in a common cause, and universal military service brought together men and women of different social backgrounds, races, ethnicities, and religions.

After the draft was eliminated in 1973 in response to the unpopular war in Vietnam, military service was no longer a universal rite of passage of young Americans. For many members of what has been called the Greatest Generation, wartime service exposed them to a wider world and broader experiences. Many of those who served as officers were college graduates and came from privileged backgrounds. A university education did not become more accessible to the working class and poor until after the war. The officers returned home from the war with enormous respect for their compatriots who came from far more modest circumstances and often lacked higher education, yet served with great courage, distinction, and intelligence. Mac had already been exposed to this broader social milieu during his summers as a ranch hand. While he attended Hotchkiss and Yale and was the son of a congressman, he always remained at heart a cowboy from Nebraska. He retained a common touch and great respect for the workingman that endured throughout his entire life and contributed to his success in Washington. It gave him a depth of humanity, compassion, and perspective. As Commerce Secretary, he often said, "Labor can't be treated as a 'cost' . . . it must be counted as a resource." He saw workers as individuals and human beings, not as commodities or assets.

Mac's combat experience seared him as it did so many of his peers, yet he rarely spoke of it. This was characteristic of his generation. As soon as the war ended in 1945, he and his fellow soldiers, sailors, marines, and airmen looked to the future, rarely speaking in any detail of what happened during the war. World War II, however, was the largest and most violent conflict in the history of mankind. It truly defined a generation, and its impact on Mac cannot be ignored.

He wrote a memoir, in his spare, straightforward prose, describing forty-seven brutal days between April 8, 1945, and May 25, 1945, battling the Japanese for control of Okinawa, the largest of the Ryukyu Islands. He called it *A Short Sojourn in the Sunny Ryukyus*, an ironic title for a gritty and explicit description of combat. The long war would finally end that August, just a week after the United States dropped the second of two atomic bombs on Japanese cities. That spring, however, the Japanese military were ferocious in routinely sending their soldiers on suicidal missions against the Americans. The toll on Mac's 27th Infantry Unit, a New York National Guard unit that had been federalized in 1942, was horrible: 1,512 killed in action, and 4,980 wounded, 332 of whom later died from their injuries. A neighboring company had gone into Tsugen Jima with 140 men but only 20 were left. At least 40 replacements had come and gone, making the casualty rate for a single month a staggering 120 percent.

Mac was a forward observer for the field artillery, an extremely dangerous position; the job required him to move ahead of the infantry forces to spot the enemy positions and then convey explicit information to the officers to direct the ground soldiers' aim. In those fateful forty-seven days, he describes the deaths of his fellow officers, one after the other. This expanded his responsibilities as he stepped up to take on their jobs. The recent college graduate carried a pistol, submachine gun, radios, and other gear that weighed more than sixty-five pounds as he climbed up rocky hills and dug into muddy foxholes under mortar fire. He shot Japanese out of caves where they hid and described the stench of the decomposing bodies of the fallen enemy left behind in the caves. In clear, concise sentences, he described scrambling for cover under machine gun fire; falling into an exhausted sleep while lying in a pool of muddy water in a fox hole he dug himself; and being too exhausted to move or react or feel the horror of his experiences.

His experience in Okinawa was curiously removed from events in the rest of the world. As the U.S. and Japanese soldiers fought to the death over that rocky island, President Franklin D. Roosevelt died on April 12; the Allies claimed victory in the European war on May 8; and the Japanese withdrew from China on May 20. Yet Mac mentions none of these significant events, perhaps because he was cut off from the rest of the world. He communicated with his family through the army postal service, and there was precious little letter writing going on for that period of time. There were no satellite phones, no Internet, no live cable news, and no Skype back then.

Combat presents soldiers with stark choices in the heat of combat, when survival is the only goal. Mac describes the split-second decision that another officer made when about thirty civilian women dressed in shawls and dresses approached them up a hill at 2:30 in the morning. The American soldiers dropped a grenade close to them to scare them away, and the "women" turned out to be Japanese soldiers who ripped off their skirts as they scattered, but not before killing a few U.S. soldiers. He writes of blasting away a Japanese shack just moments after an Okinawan woman entered it carrying ammunition. "In a case like that it was just too bad that it had to be a woman, as we had no other choice but to shoot the house down," he wrote. Confronted with an enemy intent upon killing him, Mac did what was necessary to survive, and he killed quite a few enemy combatants. He considered himself lucky, a view shared by many combat soldiers from many wars. His description of those six weeks reveals that a few inches, a ten-second delay, a different choice of a path, could have gotten him killed as well.

The occupation of Japan after hostilities ended required a switch in tactics and engagement with the civilian Japanese population that many soldiers may have found impossible. Many years later, Mac wrote an op-ed piece for the *Washington Post* in which he said he had worried whether some of his soldiers could make the switch from combatants to victors and occupiers without taking it out on the civilians. He had the advantage of education and sophistication and was able to make the transition. One minute he was fighting for his life, the next he was developing an enduring friendship with his Japanese landlady, Mama-san, a widow with children who ran the old-fashioned Japanese country inn, the Hotel Mukaitaki, in Aizu Wakamatsu, the northern town where he was assigned during the Occupation. He said his soldiers, like himself, immediately felt compassion for the people of the village. The only people left in the town were women, old men, and children, and years of Japanese propaganda had left them terrified of the Americans, who were portrayed in propaganda posters as long-nosed, white devils with bristling mustaches. The soldiers gave the children candy and purchased souvenirs from the civilians. There were no problems, said Mac, whose appearance gave the Japanese pause. He had a long nose and a handlebar mustache and bore a disturbing resemblance to the white devils in those posters. The duality of this experience informed his dealings with the Japanese many years later, both at Scovill and as Commerce Secretary. And his experience in this unusual billet gave him a lifelong love of a good soak in a hot bath.

Mac was a person of strong character, and his cowboy experiences toughened him both physically and mentally. He suffered from Marie-Strumpell Disease (*ankylosing spondylitis*), a chronic inflammatory disease of the axial skeleton that gradually fused his spine. The rare disease, believed to be genetic in origin, causes excruciating pain. When he went to enlist in the military during World War II, he was suffering from a flare-up of painful arthritis in his spine that left him hobbling on crutches. At the door of the enlistment office, he handed his crutches to a friend, gritted his teeth and pulled himself upright, then went in and toughed out the physical. Upon leaving and after successfully hoodwinking the doctors, he retrieved the crutches.

Midge told another story after Mac's death that shows his tough-mindedness and a direct no-nonsense style that were much in evidence in Washington. After their marriage, he was the foundry superintendent at Eberhard Manufacturing in Cleveland, which made auto parts and specialty hardware. "The molders at Eberhard had been staging sporadic and irresponsible, or so Mac deemed them, sit-down strikes just as the furnace was to be tapped," she said. "If the molders refused to pour the iron, it would fuse and ruin the furnace. Mac had gotten his workers to promise to allow him to work out their grievances before striking, but to cover all his bets, he prepared for a showdown by alerting the office to man hoses at a predetermined signal. When the workers did not advise Mac before striking as they had promised, he gave the signal for the hoses, dropped the bottom of the furnace, and two tons of molten iron hit the floor. Every window in the foundry broke and fifty years of soot on the rafters came down, scaring the daylights out of everybody. Hosing down the iron prevented a major fire, and there were no further strikes. Ten years later, Mac was the company president."

While probably too restless to settle down in an office upon his discharge from the army, Mac considered graduate school when he returned home. According to his daughter Megan, he was turned down by Harvard Business School. Returning veterans overwhelmed colleges and universities, and Harvard likely had filled up its class. The GI Bill gave many returning veterans from modest financial backgrounds the opportunity to attend college for the first time. So Mac went straight to work and eventually became convinced that real jobs taught him more than he could have learned in a classroom studying business theory. He had a lifelong disdain for the MBAs who never left their offices to find out what was happening on the factory floor.

During World War II, virtually every able man and boy served in the military. They put their lives and educations on hold for years so when the war ended and they came home, there was tremendous desire for normalcy and pressure to make up for lost time. The marriage rate skyrocketed, along with the number of births, creating the famous "baby boom" generation whose members would grow up and remake culture and society into their own image decades later.

Mac met Margaret Trowbridge Murray, universally known as Midge, at a wedding supper in Pittsburgh. Mutual friends were getting married. Mac arrived hours late from Cleveland where a balky foundry furnace had delayed his departure. A family story says that his toast went on so long that Midge had to curtail hers.

Midge was born in Pittsburgh in 1927, the daughter of Mary Trowbridge Murray and Lawrence Newbold Murray. Her father was the president of Mellon Bank, a major institution that financed much of the mass production revolution in the Midwest. She grew up in comfort. The family had a weekend house in horse country in Pennsylvania. The Murrays were close to the Mellon family, which included Andrew W.

Mellon, the longest serving Treasury secretary in history. Even educated women and girls had limited options throughout the first half of the twentieth century. Midge, like her friends, was expected to grow up to be someone's wife and mother. Her outlet was horseback riding. She enjoyed the freedom, excitement, and independence of riding, and she became an expert horsewoman and jumper.

She also received an excellent education. Her parents sent her to a progressive grade school in Pittsburgh. During high school, she and a contingent of Pittsburgh friends attended Chatham Hall, a fine boarding school for girls in Chatham, Virginia, with a riding program. She loved school and excelled academically. She went to Smith College, another prestigious women's school, where she studied ancient Greek, English, and zoology. After graduating from Smith in 1949, she moved to New York City, where she worked as a secretary at Oxford University Press. This was a typical career path for well-educated young ladies of means in those days. While they may have had the same skills, brains, and ambitions as their male peers, the widespread assumption was that they went to college to earn their "Mrs." degrees.

Women stepped up to take the place of men who went off to combat during the war, but as soon as the war ended and the men returned to their old jobs, women resumed traditional supporting roles in both business and at home. Most young women did not question this. It was the way things were.

Midge, though, developed her own interests and causes, including a passionate commitment to reproductive rights, and pursued them with energy and enthusiasm. In navigating the political waters in Washington, Midge could be just as blunt as Mac. When solicited to renew the annual membership with the Citizens Association of Georgetown (CAG), the neighborhood organization in the tony Georgetown neighborhood where they had bought a townhouse, she wrote a terse response explaining that they were moving out of the neighborhood because dirt and drunks had convinced them to sell the 33rd Street house. The forty-one-word note was leaked to the *Washington Post* and created a bit of a flurry. But the Citizens Association of Georgetown proposed her for honorary membership when their long-standing request for more police protection on weekends was approved, traffic improved, and the city streets were cleaned in advance of a Friday-night visit by the mayor. "Nothing like the trenchant indignation of the politically powerful to get things changed," tartly observed the writer of the CAG newsletter.

Midge felt strongly about women having control over their personal reproductive choices. The birth control pill became widely available in the 1960s after the 1965 Supreme Court in *Griswold v. Connecticut* ruled illegal the state law that prohibited married couples from using birth control. A second decision a few years later struck down the Massachusetts state law that prohibited dispensation of birth control devices to unmarried women. These decisions changed the lives of the upcoming generation of women who, for the first time, had the ability to control if and when they would have children.

Her longtime support for reproductive rights was completely at odds with the socially conservative antiabortion position of many of the most ardent Reaganites. She was alarmed when an antiabortion educational film called *The Silent Scream* was released in 1984. The movie was even shown at the White House, where the president said the film ought to be shown to every single member of Congress and Supreme Court justice. The film using ultrasound showed an abortion of a fetus. While supporters of a woman's right to choose called it misleading and manipulative, the grisly, slow-motion footage was powerful. Midge corresponded with abortion rights advocates on ways to counter the propaganda film.

Midge never expressed resentment that a conventional marriage may have limited her career opportunities, and her commitment to the prochoice cause was shared by many of her peers. They did not have many lifestyle options, but they wanted to make certain their daughters and other young women did. She was a lifelong and active member of Planned Parenthood and the National Abortion Rights League (NARAL). She maintained her commitment during the conservative Reagan years, but in deference to her husband's position in the cabinet of a prolife president, she was lower key in the choices she made as a public persona. Molly remembers her mother organizing a fund-raiser for abortion rights in Washington. Midge stayed in the kitchen preparing trays of hors d'oeuvres and sent Molly out to serve, so that reporters would not pick up on the fact that the Commerce Secretary's wife was sponsoring the fund-raiser.

Midge also took on the cause of saving the aquarium that had been located for fifty years in the basement of the 14th Street Commerce Department headquarters. Her interest in the aquarium was sparked by an early visit to the department. Midge had been told that Paul O'Day, a career government employee who had worked for decades at Commerce, had become something of a historian for the Commerce Department building. So she asked him to take her on a tour. Craig Phillips, who had been director since the 1960s and was devoted to the facility, ran the aquarium. But it was slated for a budgetary shutdown in 1982. Not only was it the sort of project that invariably got defunded in the tight-fisted Office of Management and Budget director David Stockman's budgets, but Senator Charles "Mac" Mathias, a Republican from Maryland, had already earmarked money to build a new national aquarium in Baltimore. O'Day says that Midge was initially not very interested in seeing the aquarium, but he made sure Craig Phillips was available to show her the facility. Two hours after O'Day casually steered her toward the aquarium and the administrator gave her a tour, Midge emerged a huge fan.

The facility had opened in 1885 and had been located in the dark basement of the Commerce Department since 1932, and Midge became determined to save it. She created a National Aquarium Society, a nonprofit group of cabinet wives, and they solicited private donations to operate the aquarium, sponsored an "adopt a fish" fund-raising drive, and suggested a modest admission charge to help subsidize operations. The aquarium remained open to the public for the next thirty years. It was finally closed on September 30, 2013, because of renovations at the Commerce Building, and the fish and other animals were transferred to the National Aquarium in Baltimore that opened in 1981 and had become a major tourist attraction. The National Aquarium Society still exists, and plans are being made to create an "ocean embassy" in Washington, D.C., a sort of satellite to the Baltimore facility.

Midge loved the outdoor country life and physical activity. She was the first woman to become a volunteer firefighter in the Woodbury (Connecticut) Fire Department. She deeply appreciated the volunteers' diligence and skill in battling a fire at their colonial house. A Baldrige farmhand, a member of the department, was regularly being called to fight fires, and Midge decided to join him one day. She enjoyed it and submitted her firefighter application. The town was small enough that no one dared object to Mrs. Baldrige's unusual act. The Woodbury Volunteer Fire Department had its first female member, with Midge paving the way for more women to join. After Mac's death and her return to Woodbury, she rejoined the Fire Department as a board member.

An avid knitter, Midge raised sheep for wool as well as meat. She was an organic gardener long before the term became common and maintained a victory garden in Washington with Sue Block, the wife of Agriculture Secretary John R. (Jack) Block. She was a longtime member of the League of Women Voters and monitored town finance meetings. A young reporter remembers spotting a woman quietly knitting at the back of the room during a prolonged and dreary discussion of a town issue. When the woman spoke up to ask a question or make an observation (as she continued to knit), the reporter said the meeting stopped, everyone leaned in to listen, and the dynamic of the meeting completely changed. That was Midge, who, like her husband, was a quiet, effective, and pragmatic force.

While she was five years younger than Mac, they shared many friends and traveled in similar social circles. Her socially conscious mother spent months planning their 1951 wedding. They were married in a Catholic church in deference to Mac's parents. In those years, the Catholic Church had strict rules about marrying someone of another faith. Her parents were Episcopalian, a religion with a slightly more flexible attitude. Mac and Midge raised their daughters as Congregationalists, a Protestant sect with a history of social reform. They went on a honeymoon to Guatemala, a hint that this couple was meant to have a more exciting life than those who opted for Bermuda or Niagara Falls, the popular honeymoon destinations at the time. The newlyweds moved to Cleveland, where Mac was working for the Eastern Malleable Iron Company, which produced iron and steel products. Mac had poured iron and made molds for two years at the foundry in Cleveland after the war. He wanted to learn the industry from the bottom up. By the time of their marriage, he was superintendent of the foundry machine shop. Midge said she used enormous kegs of soap to get his socks clean and wondered at times exactly what she had got herself into. Company executives asked him to take over an underperforming plant in Syracuse, New York, and they moved to upstate New York not long after their marriage. Six years later, he was promoted to vice president and moved to the headquarters office in Naugatuck, Connecticut. He became company president three years later, in 1960. Two years later, Scovill hired him as executive vice president. A year later, in 1963, he became president and CEO. It was a steady ascent.

Mac developed a clear philosophy of business. In the 1950s and 1960s, a lot of major manufacturing concerns were still closely held, if not family owned, and stuck to the old-fashioned traditional values of the founders. The older generation believed in hard work; starting at the bottom; learning the business on the factory floor; and regular investment in people, products, and research and development.

Mac was heavily influenced by the work of W. Edwards Deming, an American statistician and engineer, who developed a management method called Fourteen Points. Deming believed that improving quality would reduce expenses and increase productivity and market share. He did not find many followers in the United States in the 1950s, when American businesses had little competition and had grown exponentially in those postwar prosperous years, but he was embraced in Japan after the war. He taught a generation of top Japanese business managers how to improve their designs and services, product quality, testing, and sales. Belatedly, the value of his philosophy was recognized in the United States. President Reagan presented him with a National Medal of Technology in 1987, six years before he died at the age of ninety-three.

In those days, *politician* was not a dirty word. Elected public officials were esteemed and respected as community leaders. In Connecticut, Mac maintained his close ties to the Republican Party as a national party delegate in 1968, 1972, and 1976. The Northeast Republicans were loosely described as "Rockefeller Republicans," after New York governor Nelson Rockefeller, a preeminent leader of that wing of the GOP in those days. (Rockefeller served as the appointed vice president to Gerald R. Ford after Richard Nixon's resignation in 1974.) Rockefeller Republicans were business focused and moderately conservative on fiscal matters but progressive reformers on most social issues, particularly reproductive rights, a favorite cause of many Republican women, including Midge Baldrige. Mac made a move toward becoming a candidate himself in 1970, when he was in his late forties. At that time, party elders determined the party nominees for major state officers, who were then ratified by a nominating convention. Mac put himself forward as a candidate for governor but became the establishment's candidate for lieutenant governor instead. While the party elite met privately in one of those proverbial smoke-filled backrooms to select the slate of candidates, T. Clark Hull, a popular and engaging party leader, kept the convention entertained. When time came to announce the candidate for lieutenant governor, the convention, well oiled by alcohol, tired from the long wait, and utterly charmed by T. Clark Hull, spontaneously nominated Hull instead. It was a disappointment to Mac and a lesson in the vagaries and uncertainties of elective office. Four years later, party leaders approached him about running against popular U.S. senator Abraham Ribicoff, but Mac declined, pleading the press of business at Scovill. Mac, though, remained active in the party as a fund-raiser and power broker.

He was not an obvious choice for Commerce Secretary because he was not a Reagan man, nor was he known as a supply-side fiscal conservative, the prevailing view of the Reagan team. He had invariably supported the more moderate candidate for the Republican presidential nomination in previous elections. His candidate in 1980, George H. W. Bush, the son of a U.S. senator, had been born in Massachusetts and raised in Connecticut, but came of age in Texas. Bush's more moderate views were akin to Mac's. Moreover, the Bush and Baldrige families had been traveling in the same circles for many years. Their fathers were members of the Yale Class of 1918, and both belonged to Skull and Bones, one of Yale's senior societies, sometimes called secret societies. Nancy Bush Ellis, the sister of George H. W. Bush, was a classmate of Mac's sister Letitia at Miss Porter's School and later at Vassar, where they roomed together. George Bush's brother Prescott was a classmate of Mac's at Yale along with Nancy's future husband, Alexander "Sandy" Ellis. Mac and George Bush became great friends over the years because of their mutual interest in politics.

In 1980, Mac helped Bush win the Republican presidential primary in Connecticut, at a pivotal moment for Bush's campaign. David Broder, the longtime "dean" of the Washington press corps and a highly respected *Washington Post* reporter and columnist, described that primary as do or die for George Bush and said his victory put him back in the presidential race. The victory kept the Bush candidacy alive long enough to get Bush considered and then chosen as Reagan's vice president. Reagan gave his vice president one cabinet pick: Commerce Secretary. Mac could have been seen as an outsider in the Reagan administration among the political appointees who came to Washington with the former California governor and had worked hard on his national campaign. Indeed, many of the political veterans from the Reagan campaign were initially suspicious of him. But from the start, Mac and the new president hit it off, and Mac quickly became a favorite of both staff and his colleagues in the cabinet.

While Reagan was more conservative than Mac on some issues, they discovered they shared a similar pragmatic world-view. The two men bonded over their mutual love of cowboys, riding, and all things western. But more importantly, they shared a similar sensibility. Reagan, a former movie actor who rose to prominence as a politically conservative tide rose in the United States, was surprisingly pragmatic for someone scorned as an ideologue by his opponents and celebrated for years after his death as a conservative icon. Mac, routinely described as a "moderate conservative" in news accounts, was no ideologue. He was a doer, a practical man. He came to play a crucial role in the Reagan cabinet as the person who could, after vigorous debate, articulate a consensus position that reflected the president's inclination, philosophy, and comfort level. In an administration that included more than its share of passionate conservatives and outsized egos, he was the one who invariably found the way to compromise and move ahead.

Mac never betrayed a hint of pretension. In a city where officials were driven around in a black Cadillac or dark blue Lincoln Town Car, he was shuttled from Commerce to the White House in a red Mercury sedan. Initially, Mac also had the standard-issue black car. After he left a White House meeting and climbed into the wrong black car, he insisted on a car that he could readily identify from others in the fleet of black luxury vehicles. This down-to-earth quality endeared him to others. Eight months after he took office, a senior White House aide in *U.S. News & World Report*'s popular Washington Whispers column identified Mac as the second most influential member of the Reagan cabinet after Treasury Secretary Donald Regan. A Newhouse News Service article in 1981 explained, "Baldrige is blunt, which seems to hold more appeal for the President than the styles of " other economic advisers.

At cabinet meetings, Mac kept his own counsel most of the time, a fairly unusual strategy in a room full of strong per-

sonalities and successful men who were accustomed to dominating discussions and getting their way. So when he did
speak, others listened. Senior staff members who attended
cabinet meetings said that Mac often summed up the arguments pro and con for the president at the conclusion of a
discussion among the cabinet members. He had an instinct
for creative compromise, and his practical business background caused him to focus on problem solving. He is credited for finding a sensible middle ground on the trade wars
then beginning to rage between "free traders" and "protectionists." This alternative approach came to be known as "fair
trade," a careful strategy that kept trade flowing in and out of
the United States but also forced trading partners to follow
the rules, while giving U.S. business the chance to compete.
In this way, he exerted influence far beyond the legal powers
of his office.

Mac majored in English literature at Yale and wrote
his senior thesis on Chaucer. He said he picked English as
a major because the English reading list was better than
the reading lists of other subjects. He had an enduring
resistance to obfuscation in language. He preferred clear,
clean prose and eventually became well known for his edict
that Commerce Department employees write letters and
memos in a style "halfway between Zane Grey and Ernest
Hemingway." Zane Grey was a popular Western novelist, and
Ernest Hemingway was one of the great novelists of the twentieth century who used short sentences and spare prose. Mac
had an unlimited appetite for the Western novels of Zane
Grey and Louis L'Amour. Both novelists were prolific and
churned out dozens of novels about the rough life on the
Western frontier. Mac said he liked their books because he
could read them in the tub and not worry if the paperback
fell into the bath water. Indeed, the bottom halves of most

of Mac's Western paperbacks were fatter than the top halves, indicating a propensity to nod off in the tub after a long day.

As a follower of Deming's management philosophy, he believed in investment, modernization, ongoing research and development, and a decent benevolent policy toward employees as the ways to maintain a competitive edge. While there were still many business leaders who shared his viewpoint, they were fast becoming viewed as a bit old-fashioned and quickly becoming a dying breed. The focus on short-term profits and quarterly gains by investors and Wall Street bankers and traders was beginning to erode this view. Investors' short-sighted, razor focus on quarterly profits put unacceptable strains on many businesses that felt pressured to sacrifice long-term investment to short-term gain. Mac's standing as the former executive of a billion-dollar-a-year company gave him the right to criticize business, and while he was seen as the most prominent friend of business in Washington, he did not shy away from calling management on the carpet for poor management practices. He once called American management "fat, dumb and happy." Moreover, he had the credibility to do so—an unusual dual role of supporter and critic of American business at a time when global economies were in flux. This set the stage for the new president, his administration, and his Commerce Secretary, as Mac and Midge headed to Washington.

2

FIRST YEAR
IN THE CABINET

RONALD REAGAN TOOK OFFICE AT A PIVOTAL MOMENT FOR the United States and its economy. The United States had emerged virtually unscathed from World War II compared to its allies and enemies. Geography protected the country; two enormous oceans on either side kept its cities and population safe from enemy bombs. In addition, the United States had entered the worldwide conflict several years after other countries, so it had not needed to shoulder the daunting costs of war for as long a period of time. While the nation went into a wartime mode and every citizen was expected to serve, the sacrifice of Americans, however meritorious, did not come close to the years of deprivation, the millions of deaths, and the heartbreak and devastation that leveled much of Europe and Japan.

Most of Europe and major cities in the Soviet Union (the Union of Soviet Socialist Republics or USSR) and Japan were on their heels—exhausted, depleted, and in many cases very nearly destroyed from years of a devastating war. Nearly every major European city sustained horrific damage from the bombs of the world's first real air war. Industrial facilities and the transportation infrastructure were particularly hard hit. Virtually every factory, bridge, road, airport, and transportation hub in Western Europe had been damaged or destroyed. Japan was even worse off. The U.S. atomic bomb obliterated two major cities, Hiroshima and Nagasaki. In Hiroshima, 69 percent of the buildings were completely destroyed by "Fat Boy," the first atomic bomb, and about 40 percent of the city's population was killed instantly. Another 20 percent of the citizenry died of injuries and radiation poisoning within a year. U.S. and Allied bombs also wiped out 40 percent of Japan's industrial plants and infrastructure.

After the final shots were fired, the United States was the world's only superpower in every sense, particularly economic. The United States stepped up to help its allies with the European Recovery Program, known as the Marshall Plan, named after Secretary of State George Marshall. The goal was to rebuild Europe's economy, eliminate trade barriers, and modernize industry. The five-year program funneled $13 billion (roughly $125 billion in today's money) into Europe, and by 1952 the participating countries had resumed or surpassed their prewar levels of production.

In Japan, the United States became the occupying power with total control over the government and industry for seven years, from 1945 to 1952. The purposes of the occupation were to reduce the power of the monarchy; replace a militaristic government with a true democracy; and eliminate the social, cultural, and governmental institutions that had contributed to the war. To create a democracy, American planners at the State Department realized they had to rebuild the economy. They used the United States as the economic model.

The United States was not just being benevolent when it provided massive aid to Japan and Europe. There was plenty of self-interest. Rebuilding Europe and Japan would create markets for U.S. goods. The motivation was also political, because the principal policymakers were at the State Department. In their view, a strong Western Europe and democratic Japan were needed to offset the growing threat of international communism. American policymakers fixated on containing the spread of communism and maintaining a balance of power that would forestall World War III. A strong Western Europe would keep the USSR at bay; a reinvigorated and democratic Japan was seen as a counterweight to Communist China in Asia. Mao Zedong, the Communist revolutionary, founded the People's Republic of China in 1949. When it became clear that Mao was a Communist, General Douglas MacArthur, the five-star army general who was the Supreme Commander for the Allied Powers and effectively the dictator of Japan after the war, shifted recovery efforts away from democratic reforms and toward rebuilding Japan's shattered economy. A democratic Japan with trading partners throughout the world was less likely to engage in the aggression of the past. While the German war machine had been cut off at its knees by the military defeat, these policymakers reasoned that economically strong countries around Germany would reduce the odds of a Nazi-like effort rising again to threaten the international order. The State Department and its diplomats called the shots, and for decades their views and priorities would color the U.S. international economic dealings and trade policy.

Although Russia had been an important ally of the United States and Western Europe during the war, the alliance was always a shaky one and did not survive the peace. Joseph Stalin, a Communist and the Russian leader, had entered into a nonaggression pact with Adolf Hitler in 1939, fully intent upon staying out of Europe's fight. But Hitler violated the pact and invaded Poland, bringing the USSR into the war on the Allies' side. There was a tremendous amount of suspicion between the Russians and the Allies. The agents of the Office of Strategic Services (OSS), the intelligence arm of the U.S. military and forerunner of the CIA, were spying on their Russian allies even before the war ended. Russia began to reinforce its own buffer zone and region of influence in Eastern Europe and got the West to agree, in two major postwar agreements, at Yalta and Potsdam. Those agreements never led to friendship. Once the USSR got the atomic bomb, the game was set. The "Iron Curtain," a rhetorical term that characterized the division between East and West, came to define the era of the Cold War. Political careers in the United States were made and lost over who was perceived as tougher on the communists. As the years passed, the United States and the USSR engaged in proxy battles for influence throughout the world and battled for primacy through a costly arms race. From the vantage point of 2014, with the knowledge of the internal weaknesses of the Soviet Union, it is difficult to appreciate how terrified Americans were of the communist menace for so long. Many people viewed communism as nothing short of a dire threat to the American way of life. Of course, by 1980, the USSR was beginning to collapse from the pressure of that expensive battle, the limitations of a closed economic system, and widespread corruption. When Reagan took office, however, this was not apparent. Indeed, the signs of Soviet economic and political stress were largely missed in the West, and the eventual collapse of the USSR caught even longtime U.S. spies by surprise.

So in 1980 and 1981, the Soviet Union and Red China were still our enemies, and international communism was still viewed as the most formidable threat to the United States.

Reagan, the former movie actor, played the part of the Cold Warrior to the hilt, notably during a famous speech on June 12, 1987, at the Berlin Wall when he exhorted Soviet leader Mikhail Gorbachev to "tear down this wall." He began to apply more pressure to the USSR by increasing U.S. military spending, which forced the Soviet Union to respond in kind in an attempt to keep pace.

While the Cold War between the United States and the USSR dominated international policy, the Europeans, freed of the need to spend much government money on defense because of the North Atlantic Treaty Organization (NATO), focused on rebuilding their economies. Europe's economy surpassed its prewar economic condition. NATO kept the United States and our deep pockets engaged in the defense of Europe. Japan was forbidden from engaging in any overseas military action, so a larger portion of its resources also went into rebuilding its domestic economy. Japan had another key advantage: the world's highest literacy rate and highest educational standards after World War II. With the economy beginning to put more value on brains than brawn, and as new technology sectors began to grow, Japan was unusually well positioned to prosper. Japan wasted no time in building upon its inherent strengths—a strong culture of discipline and shared sacrifice, and its hard-working traditions—to create what became known in the 1980s as Japan Inc., an economic powerhouse whose economy rivaled and threatened to surpass its onetime enemy, the United States.

By 1980, Europe and Japan had not only returned to economic vigor, but they were posing a significant threat to the United States' longtime primacy in world markets. European governments, many with democratic socialist traditions, routinely subsidized key industries and provided help to manufacturers. As time went on, several European countries would join together on major projects, such as the production of a new generation of airplanes to compete with the sleek and expensive aircraft made in the United States. The United States embraced a more laissez-faire tradition in economics, almost a Darwinian survival-of-the-fittest mentality that dated back to its earliest days as a proving ground for ambitious capitalists and self-made men. While the U.S. government also provided tax breaks, subsidies, and incentives to domestic businesses, its assistance was less overt, prompting U.S. industries to cry foul when foreign nations provided blatant domestic subsidies allowing their manufacturers to beat U.S. prices.

Mac Baldrige understood that foreign competition was only one issue facing American business. He had a sophisticated understanding of the nation's industrial base. He had worked his way up to the top from the factory floor, which gave him insight into how things were made and how to manage people and encourage them to do their best. He believed that the postwar economic primacy had made U.S. industries complacent, even lazy. They had not had to battle their way to the top of international markets. In the absence of significant competition, supremacy in those markets had almost been handed to them. The new generation of money managers, making fortunes on Wall Street, was intent upon reaping quarterly profits and rewarding companies that produced short-term gains. Long-term investments, the sort of investments that the Europeans and Japanese had sacrificed to make in the early postwar years, were viewed as too expensive and unnecessary. This thinking was proving to be "penny wise and pound foolish."

At the same time, the foundations of the nation's economy were beginning to change. The Industrial Revolution that began in Britain in the nineteenth century had exploded in the United States, where raw materials, labor, land, and opportunities were greater. This industrial and manufacturing base of the U.S. economy was shifting to a knowledge

and service base by the 1980s. The collapse of domestic
manufacturing, involving companies that made everything
from television sets to shoes, was dramatic. Factory after factory closed, many in one-industry towns in New England and
the Midwest. As manufacturing plants moved, first to the
American South where antiunion "right to work" state laws
kept wages lower, and then to developing low-wage countries
overseas, the factory jobs that paid enough to support a family disappeared, leaving severe economic dislocation behind.
The replacement jobs for those with limited formal education
paid only a fraction of the old jobs. More than one factory
worker with a union wage job and benefits ended up flipping
hamburgers at a fast food chain restaurant for the minimum
wage and no health insurance, vacation, or pension. Once
robust downtown retail centers closed for lack of business.
The high-tech revolution was in its infancy, but it was becoming apparent that higher education and specialized training
would be essential to achieve economic success in the future.
And finally, the globe was shrinking. Globalization was not a
term used much in those days, but it had become very clear
that modernity and technology were shrinking the size of
the world and creating new markets and opportunities for
up-and-coming producers. In these first years of a globalized
economy, international trade was more important than ever.

Therefore, when Ronald Reagan took office in January
1981, the global status quo that had endured since the end
of World War II was cracking. There was an uneasy sense that
the United States was lagging behind. A number of factors
contributed to this apprehension. The proxy war against the
communists in Vietnam had been enormously unpopular in
the United States and ended in 1975 with what was seen as
the first loss of a war by the United States. Losing a war dealt
a psychic blow to a country that had always "won." The resignation of President Richard M. Nixon in the summer of 1974

in the midst of the Watergate scandal fostered skepticism of government and politicians, and it led to the election of an outsider as president in 1976, Jimmy Carter, a one-term governor from Georgia. Carter only served one term as president because of inexperience and a dose of bad luck. He injected a new emphasis on human rights into foreign policy, which was grievously unpopular with the anticommunist hardliners, including Democrats like Washington state senator Henry "Scoop" Jackson, who viewed the human rights focus as a sign of weakness. Moreover, Carter held office at a time of an international oil shortage, created by the Middle Eastern oil-producing countries that manipulated world markets for profit. The fuel shortage hit the most economically advanced countries the hardest because of their dependence upon fossil fuels to maintain modern lifestyles. The shortage put inflationary pressure on the economy and caused interest rates to soar into the double digits, thereby pricing homes and major purchases out of reach for many middle-income people. After President Carter agreed to a request by David Rockefeller and other friends of the shah of Iran to allow the deposed shah to enter the United States for medical treatment, enraged Iranian militants stormed and seized the U.S. embassy in Tehran, taking more than one hundred hostages. They held half of the hostages until Ronald Reagan's inauguration day, releasing the final fifty-two hostages at the exact time Reagan took his oath of office, in a not-so-subtle snub to Carter. For many Americans, the hostage taking revealed a serious decline in U.S. might; the release of the hostages, just as Reagan was sworn into office, was taken as a sign that a strong leader was back in charge.

At the same time, the United States had just come through two decades of social turmoil and cultural change. In the 1960s and 1970s, African Americans, other minority groups, and women mounted campaigns for full rights. The civil rights movement exploded into violence in America's cities in the late 1960s after the assassinations of Martin Luther King Jr. and Robert F. Kennedy. The unpopular war in Vietnam triggered widespread public demonstrations and disrupted college campuses from coast to coast in the first years of the 1970s. The baby boom generation was coming of age and rebelling against the style and standards of their parents. All of this turmoil left many feeling unsettled and anxious. These conditions helped fuel the political success of Ronald Reagan. His brand of conservatism was almost a nostalgic appeal to restoring the United States, its traditional culture, and its position in the world.

The Commerce Department was not the best place for making a difference in the U.S. economy. Some of the Commerce Department responsibilities dated back to the beginning of the republic. The department forecast the weather, counted citizens, assessed the state of the economy month by month, governed patents and trademarks, operated satellites, and shared responsibility for international trade with Treasury and the U.S. trade representative. A slim department history published after Mac's death and dedicated to his memory was titled *From Lighthouses to Laserbeams*. Even as satellites became part of the Commerce portfolio, the department still had responsibility for the handful of lighthouses left on the coastline. While the overall mission was clear, to promote and develop the domestic and foreign commerce of the United States, the Department itself was viewed as an unwieldy, ineffective government bureaucracy.

Even the vast size and architecture of the Department's building at 1401 Constitution Avenue, just two blocks from the White House, did not seem to fit the times. It had more hallway length than any other building in Washington, until the Pentagon was built in 1942. The building loomed over a main entry to downtown Washington from Northern Virginia, big and gray with four thousand employees, about one-tenth of the people who staffed the Department around the world. Kenneth Bacon, a *Wall Street Journal* reporter who years later would become the chief spokesman at the Pentagon, wrote that Mac found the dark, dingy entryway to the cavernous building depressing. He called the building's facilities people to ask if the entry could be spruced up, only to learn that in the government, any improvements fell under the domain of the General Services Administration, the housekeeping arm and official landlord for the federal government. It was a Welcome to Washington moment for a CEO who was accustomed to getting what he wanted in his own building.

Over the years, Congress and administrative fiat had added agencies and functions on an ad hoc basis. In the early 1980s, the Commerce Department could have been described as a polyglot of fiefdoms. At that time, the Commerce Department housed fourteen agencies, most of which had no relationship to one another. Juanita Kreps, a former Commerce Secretary, had often described the Department as a kind of Noah's Ark, with one of everything rather than two. A Scripps Howard News Service article from December 11, 1980, the day Mac's appointment was announced, noted that Mac would be inheriting agencies with a lot of problems, such as Japan's increasing success in selling cars to American motorists (the International Trade Administration), the Commerce Department's dismal track record promoting foreign tourism (the U.S. Travel and Tourism Agency), and the growing need to help depressed industrial towns develop new industries (the Economic Development Administration and the Minority Business Development Agency). The reporter wrote that Commerce had "a long and dreary reputation as a dumping ground for sleepy bureaucrats . . . Chances are that Mac Baldrige will need his roping talents and his affability to ride herd on the U.S. Commerce Department."

In the presidential cabinet, the secretaries of Treasury, State, and Defense hold the power positions by statute. These departments are officially in charge of the United States' money, diplomacy, and military. The Commerce Department had always played second fiddle; its reputation as overgrown and stodgy did not raise expectations for Mac's tenure or stature in Washington. But President Reagan, a Republican with a clear-eyed view of the government's role, wanted to make the federal government more responsive to U.S. business, and he wanted Mac to have more authority in trade and economic policy. Mac faced a management challenge and expectations deficit from the start. He needed to bring some order to this unwieldy bureaucracy while building credibility with U.S. business leaders, his president, and his colleagues in the cabinet. Luckily, he had the advantage of the president's backing.

Sometimes he was necessarily distracted from this all-important management job by the political agendas of other Departments. Mac was not known for suffering fools gladly, nor for finding any enjoyment in make-work junkets, but sometimes the job required him to grit his teeth and engage in the elaborate rituals of politics and diplomacy. Assistant Commerce Secretary James P. (Jim) Moore remembers a time when Mac was dispatched to Romania to visit its dictator Nicolae Ceausescu, a brutal and repressive communist leader. Despite the blatant violations of human rights in his own country, U.S. diplomats engaged with Ceausescu because of his independence from the Soviet Union, which allowed him to be perceived as a communist bridge to the West. To pay Romania's heavy debts, Ceausescu had most of the country's agricultural and industrial production shipped overseas. This created serious shortages and a low standard of living for Romanians. The dictator, though, maintained appearances, and on this trip, Mac and his party stayed at the only Western hotel in Bucharest, the Intercontinental.

After discovering most of the menu items were not available, Mac turned to a preening waiter to ask if he could make a good dry martini. The waiter said, "Of course we can! What would you like, red or white?" Mac seethed over the waste of his time when he realized that the dictator was only using the visit to bolster his own shaky position, but Moore reports that he kept his cool. As he left, he waved a vigorous good-bye to Romania from the top of the stairs to his official U.S. jet. His aides say they were certain he was vowing to never, ever return. After more than twenty years of repression, Ceausescu was finally ousted from power in 1989; he and his wife were shot by a firing squad after being convicted of crimes against humanity.

When Mac became CEO of Scovill, Inc., in 1963, he had faced a similar situation as the one at Commerce—an unwieldy and bloated organization. Despite the differences between the public and private sectors, Mac was able to use some of the same tactics he used streamlining a large international company to manage a cumbersome government bureaucracy in Washington. In 1963, Scovill had sales of $169.3 million and profits of $4.4 million. To improve the sales to nearly $1 billion by 1980, Mac streamlined the chain of command, cut salary overhead by $3 million, and established a young, strong management team. His global management headquarters totaled seventy people, including support staff. His management philosophy put a premium on direct and uncluttered lines of authority, with individual responsibility and decision capabilities extended as far down the line as possible. This empowered individual employees, even at relatively low levels of the firm, and gave individuals pride of ownership in their jobs. He often said that committees did not make decisions at Scovill, individual people did. He did not micromanage; he delegated responsibility to employees and encouraged them to perform.

Mac was the quintessential CEO in that respect. The first time he spoke to Commerce Department employees in the building auditorium, he introduced himself, listed his five top priorities, and then introduced his deputy, Joe Wright. He walked off the stage and left Joe to run the rest of the meeting. Joe said he was surprised by his boss's abrupt departure from the podium, but it proved to be a characteristic element of Mac's style. He expected his people to do their jobs and gave them the room and the authority to work.

When Mac took over Commerce, the Department had an annual budget of $3.421 billion and 31,249 employees, a number that ballooned to about fifty thousand every ten years when the Commerce Department took the national census. Some 60 percent of the total budget went to two agencies: the Economic Development Administration (EDA), which awarded loans and grants to foster job creation, and the National Oceanic and Atmospheric Administration (NOAA). The transition document prepared by knowledgeable insiders for the new Reagan administration was blunt in its characterization of the Department. While the Commerce Department was perceived as the federal agency responsible for business promotion, it could not really be an effective advocate because of a lack of legal authority. "As a result of its impotence, the Department is statutorily incapable of achieving its bloated mission. A new Secretary who does not realize the Department's inherent limitations is likely to look foolish by pronouncing his priorities. More than likely, these intentions will be frustrated by a lack of authority to deliver meaningful results," said the report.

This gloomy report must have been disheartening to the new Commerce Secretary. While EDA grants and loans were boons to specific cities, states, and businesses, and NOAA did important scientific charting and forecasting work for skies and seas, Mac did not see himself in

Washington to monitor Doppler radar systems or regulate numbers of fishing days. The transition document identified an opportunity for the new Secretary. "Perhaps the greatest opportunity for departmental significance at present lies in its international trade responsibilities. Many of them were recently transferred from other agencies as part of an effort to enhance programs that supposedly contribute to U.S. trade competitiveness. The greatest risk with emphasis on the Department's international trade role, is, again, one of authority. The current mix of programs and those that might be targeted on trade problems are likely to have modest results in comparison to such developments as changing currency values or energy independence."

Mac wasted little time in making changes where he could. The Department had an enormous policy division that reported directly to him. More than eighty people came up with ideas and plans that had largely stayed on the shelf in previous administrations. The policy shop acted as a powerful palace guard; every initiative had to go through that department. Otto Wolff, who served in several capacities under Mac, said, "Mac did not believe in a bunch of second guessers on the fifth floor [where the Secretary's Office is located]." He expected his key managers to manage their own shops and report to him. He eliminated the wonky policy shop. He gave the U.S. Maritime Administration, which maintains the National Defense Reserve Fleet of ships for national emergencies, to the Department of Transportation. This was an unusual step. Cabinet secretaries typically wanted to increase their budgets, powers, and number of employees. The budgetary system in Washington encourages an acquisitive nature. But he thought the Maritime Administration was a better fit for the Transportation Department and gladly gave it away, even though the department represented 17 percent of the Commerce Department budget and 4 percent of its employees. At another time, a government reorganization proposal called for the Small Business Administration to be transferred to the Department of Commerce. Kay Bulow, an assistant secretary, remembers that Mac did not want it, and he advised her and others to avoid promoting the idea. Within a year, he had reduced the department budget by 40 percent and cut the number of employees by 25 percent. This record was unmatched by any other Cabinet Secretary and strengthened his negotiating position over future budgetary issues with David Stockman, the thirty-five-year-old enfant terrible of the administration who was the top budget slasher at the Office of Management and Budget. As a result, Mac was often able to go to the mat with the powerful OMB and get approval for his priorities.

The Secretary explained how this worked in a speech in late January 1982: "We've taken the deepest cuts in the Administration this year, which is one reason I had to have a little chat with Dave Stockman recently when OMB suggested cuts in our export development area and cuts that would have severely limited our Foreign Commercial Service. After our talk, Dave agreed and those cuts were restored so our job creating programs won't be adversely affected."

Mac's executive assistant was the formidable Helen W. Robbins, a native of Brownwood, Texas, a small town two hundred miles south of Fort Worth. She was adopted by parents who divorced when she was a toddler, and her adoptive mother raised her. Helen attended Texas Christian University for about a year and a half before leaving to work full time at an aviation company, where she met a flight operations engineer from Pratt and Whitney in Connecticut, Harold E. Robbins Jr. She married him and moved to Farmington, Connecticut. She stayed at home to raise their daughter, Ruth, but her organizational skills could not be repressed. Helen helped found the Farmington Cooperative Nursery School when she and some other mothers were dissatisfied with the other nursery school in town. She also became involved in Farmington town politics. A hard worker, a shrewd and instinctive politician, and a natural organizer, she rose steadily through the ranks of Republican politics in the state. When her marriage ended, she made a living as a GOP organizer in Connecticut and was seen as one of the top political operatives in the state. Eventually, she directed the George H. W. Bush presidential primary campaign in Connecticut in 1980.

In Connecticut and Washington, she was Mac's operational person. She was far more than a reliable right hand. A fiercely protective and loyal person, she was the junkyard dog and the gatekeeper for the Secretary. Her daughter, Ruth, says that Helen was initially worried that she did not have enough formal education to go to Washington with Mac; Ruth assured her mother that Helen's life experience was sufficient for her to excel at her job. Her title of Executive Assistant vastly understated her importance and role. She was Mac's chief of staff, a powerful one who worked as a peer with the top deputies for other cabinet secretaries. She lived the job, arriving early in the morning, staying into the evening hours, and working another six hours on Saturday. While she deliberately kept a low profile, no one in the Department doubted or questioned her authority and role.

Helen's aggressive protective posture did not always endear her to her colleagues. But because she dealt with the details, her boss could focus on the big picture. She could be brusque, but she was effective. Mac knew what he had in Helen, and she did what he wanted her to do. He knew the value of a strong gatekeeper and clearly had confidence in her.

Mac took care to identify the right managers for each important sector and did not care if a career employee was best qualified for what was deemed a "political" position. In the federal government, the civil service cadre of permanent employees keeps the government in operation year after year through changes in administration, but each president gets to name a specific number of political appointees who set the policy and tone to reflect the president, his priorities, and his political party. Mac could not just name his own people. He had to accommodate the preferences of the White House Personnel Office, the final arbiter for many political hires. White House Personnel favored its own list of job applicants, which always included individuals who supported the campaign as donors or workers.

The Commerce Department, like every other cabinet department, had its own political Personnel Office, headed first by Jo McKenzie, who was a significant fund-raiser for the Republican Party in Connecticut, and then by Mary Ann Knauss Fish. Mrs. Fish had run the Reagan-Bush Connecticut campaign under the chairmanship of Mac and former ambassador John Davis Lodge. Any political hire also had to go through this office and then pass muster with Lyn Nofziger, the Assistant to the President for Political Affairs at the White House, who made sure that the candidate had helped get Reagan elected.

Before he even took office, Mac received a computerized list of names from the Reagan personnel people for the fifteen key subcabinet jobs at Commerce. He had to accept some appointees for political reasons. Knowing exactly the type of people he wanted for other vacant positions, Mac recruited them and cleared a path for their approval with the White House. He spent weeks interviewing candidates himself. Joe Wright, the first Deputy Secretary of Commerce under Mac, had served on the Reagan transition team and intended to return to his job at Citibank in New York City when his transition role ended. On the day that Joe was scheduled to catch the shuttle back to New York, Mac invited him for a drink at the Mayflower, an elegant old hotel just blocks from the White House. Joe had given Mac a list of potential candidates for Deputy Secretary, but Mac wanted Joe to take the job. Joe demurred. Mac insisted he have another drink and kept up the pressure. After a few more martinis, Joe returned home to New York that night and told his wife, Ellen, "We are going to D.C. Monday." Joe went on to have a very successful career at the highest levels of government and finance and still says, "Mac was absolutely by far the best executive I ever worked with."

It was a challenge for Mac to measure accomplishment in a bureaucracy like the Commerce Department, where employees enjoyed the protection of either labor unions or the Civil Service or both. Mac was an advocate of management by objective. Every division and agency under his control set specific goals and ways of measuring progress toward those goals in a formal system, where the boxes would be checked and headway assessed. No one in the department particularly liked the management-by-objectives program, which entailed tedious meetings to show compliance and progress toward goals, but having that system made a difference in performance. No one could ignore a priority without being called on the carpet. Additionally, the Commerce Secretary made it crystal clear to the political appointees that he expected them to work as teammates with the career staff.

Like a good CEO, Mac was decisive and made his concerns clear. A few weeks into the new administration, some of the new hires were in conflict over roles, office space, and access to the Secretary. When he learned of these petty disputes, he called his key staff to his office for a meeting at the end of the day. About thirty people, ranging from his chef, driver, and Departmental Assistant Secretaries up to the top political appointees, gathered at his office at 5 p.m. He delivered a little speech, according to his deputy, Joe Wright.

"Mac said, 'When anyone starts a new organization you have to work a little bit to jell as a team. Sometimes that is not easy. I understand there are a few issues. This is what we are going to do: by Monday, I want you to tell me that everything has been resolved. Otherwise, I am going to take my good old hat there and put every one of your positions in it and you are going to draw a number.' He then looked at my driver, John, and said, 'Johnny, I hope you can type.' And he looked at Helen (his executive assistant and de facto chief of staff) and said, 'Helen, I hope you can drive a car.'" There was no misunderstanding his serious intent. This cowboy did not make idle threats. Wright says that all the problems were resolved quickly and without further debate.

On another occasion, his chief trade expert and legal counsel were fighting over which of them would sign a new agreement. Mac said that if they could not resolve the issue, then Joe Wright was instructed to come back in an hour and tell him which one they were going to fire, and Mac would fire one of them or both of them himself. That signature issue was promptly resolved.

Assistant Secretary Jim Moore remembered another moment when two senior political appointees got into such a heated argument that one of them stormed into Mac's office and quit his job on the spot. When he arrived home that night, his wife was horrified, reminding him of the need to pay the mortgage and their children's tuition bills. She insisted he return to work Monday to ask Secretary Baldrige for his job back. That Monday, the appointee went into a previously scheduled meeting with a Korean delegation, took a 3 × 5 inch card and wrote, "Mac, I have reconsidered and would like to remain here at the Department." He passed it down the table to the Secretary who was presiding over the meeting with the Koreans. Without missing a beat, Mac read the note, took out his pen and wrote: "Have already chosen your successor. Good luck to you."

Despite the stereotypical image of government employees, the workday in Washington proved to be much more demanding than the 9 to 5 schedule Mac was said to have followed in Waterbury, but Mac quickly adjusted to the long workdays in Washington. He was picked up in the morning by a car and driver at the small Georgetown townhouse he and Midge bought at 1310 33rd Street, sometimes as early as 6:30 so he could make a 7 a.m. breakfast meeting. He routinely worked until 7 p.m., when he might have to change clothes and join Midge at a black tie event. Many political people can spend a career in Washington and never get invited to a State Dinner, a prestigious and formal event held at the White House to honor foreign heads of state. Mac and Midge attended many of those elegant dinners, and Midge saved the engraved invitations, pasting them into the scrapbooks she maintained on their Washington years. This, too, was a big part of any cabinet officer's responsibilities: to attend numerous formal and informal cocktail parties and dinners. The contacts and conversations during these events might further diplomatic, political, or departmental work, making attendance part of a Commerce Secretary's job.

While some cabinet agencies had rooms specifically for entertaining foreign and domestic guests, Commerce, despite its enormous size, did not have anything comparable or suitable. In fact, when Mac traveled overseas, he often fretted that his hosts—who often organized dinners in elegant, well-appointed government suites loaded with antiques, plush carpeting, and exquisite silver and glassware—would not be treated equally in the United States, because the Commerce Department had no such venues nor was there much budget for entertaining foreign guests. He arranged to expand a dining room near his office and put in new carpeting. The expenditure drew negative press coverage, but the dinners and social events played a vital role in international diplomacy. Often, foreign officials' decisions on trade issues were swayed by the treatment they received and the quality of the cocktail parties and dinners. Mac was a deft enough student of human nature to understand that a little bit of extra effort, including a personal gesture, was often politically smart.

He had a personal touch that he used to great advantage. Mary Ann Fish's official job at the Commerce Department was Director of the State and Local Assistance Office, and she was responsible for solving any problem a governor or big-city mayor might have at the Department. She remembers that Mac convinced Governor Bob Orr of Indiana to lead the first state delegation overseas on a trade mission. They were great friends; Orr had attended Hotchkiss and Yale just a few years before Mac and had served in the army in the Pacific Theater during the war.

On another occasion, Mary Ann worked energetically to secure five minutes on the Secretary's schedule for a meeting with the governor of American Samoa. Republican Peter Tali Coleman was the first popularly elected governor of American Samoa, but more importantly, he served as a captain in the army on the Solomon Islands during World War II. He and Mac quickly established the wartime connection, and the five-minute stop-by turned into a lengthy and warm meeting.

As Mac was finishing up his first year as Secretary, a *Wall Street Journal* reporter asked him to describe the differences between running a billion-dollar private company and a huge cabinet department. Mac responded, "When I was in the private sector, I'd go to bed and count all the good things I helped happen that day; in the government, I count up the bad stuff I stopped from happening." But in reality, he drew upon his skills and experience to have a far greater impact than indicated by his modest "do no harm" attitude.

3

TRADE WARS

EVERY PRESIDENT TAKES OFFICE BRIMMING WITH OPTIMISM and the certainty that he and his team can tame the massive federal government and force the beast to do his bidding. Ronald Reagan was no exception.

He decided to run his cabinet like a CEO would run his executive team. The cabinet officers would advise him on how to slow the growth of government and reduce the financial and regulatory burdens that he believed government imposed on businesses and consumers. He delegated authority to them but wanted to make the major decisions himself. He set up Cabinet Councils that were smaller subgroups to focus on specific areas. Mac had positions on three Cabinet Councils, as many posts as Treasury Secretary Donald Regan, who was widely considered the most powerful member of the cabinet. Mac chaired the Cabinet Council on Commerce and Trade and served on the councils on Economic Affairs and Natural

Resources. This was duly noted in the Capital City where who is up, who is down, who is in favor, and who is not is a popular parlor game. These assignments were seen as evidence that Mac was an important player and had the president's ear.

In October 1981, Jack Nelson, a top political reporter for the *Los Angeles Times*, wrote a lengthy magazine piece assessing and ranking the cabinet members. "Traditionally considered the weak sister of Washington bureaucracy," he wrote, "Commerce under Baldrige has begun to exercise an authority unequaled perhaps since the early 1920's when then-Secretary Herbert Hoover turned the agency into a real power in Washington."

A cataclysmic event, the attempted assassination of the president, took place at the beginning of the Reagan administration. John Hinckley Jr., a mentally disturbed young man, became obsessed with the actress Jodie Foster, then a Yale freshman, who had achieved great fame playing a child prostitute in the movie *Taxi Driver*. On March 30, 1981, just two months into the administration, Hinckley shot and wounded Reagan and several others outside the Washington Hilton Hotel in an effort to impress Foster. Reagan was badly hurt and came closer to death than was acknowledged at the time. Mac's reaction was calm, measured, and practical. Joe Wright, his deputy, remembers they were meeting with a group of ambassadors discussing a trade agreement when Mac's top staffer, Helen Robbins, came in with a note saying the president had been shot. He read the note, looked up, and told the group that he had shocking news: the president had been shot and there was not yet a report on his condition. The meeting immediately ended as the ambassadors rushed back to their respective embassies. Joe remembered that he and Mac sat quietly together in the empty meeting room when Mac said, "The one thing we do not do is overreact. There will be too much of that. Let's make sure everybody settles down." His instinct was telling. At the same time, Secretary of State Alexander Haig rushed into the White House briefing room and firmly announced, "I'm in control here." Haig was widely criticized for making a power grab. Vice President George Bush was in an airplane hours away from Washington, and Haig was the fourth in line to the presidency, after Bush, the Speaker of the House, and the President Pro Tem of the Senate. One could make the argument that he was the second highest-ranking administration official in town at the time. (It was later learned that Haig made the statement to send a clear message to the Soviet Union, which wasted no time in mobilizing troops in Eastern Europe after receiving reports of the shooting. His intent was to keep the Soviets from taking advantage of any momentary confusion or perceived power vacuum in the United States.)

Mac sent Reagan a get-well note of encouragement, probably something about cowboys being tough, and Reagan responded with a note in early April. "Dear Mac: Your note struck a responsive chord, especially the part about us old cowboys, and I am trying to live up to it. Just know that you are appreciated—and very much." The note was signed "Ron" in a sign of the growing personal friendship between the two men.

Mac deftly built upon the legitimate functions of Commerce to make the most of the department's influence and raise its prestige and clout. It was clear to Mac that international trade was the one area where he might have some impact and the one economic sphere where the Commerce Department actually wielded some legal authority. The law gave the Commerce Department the power to settle trade cases involving dumping and countervailing duties. This institutional and legal responsibility put the Commerce Department squarely in the center of the biggest trade issues of the time. The Department shared responsibility for trade with the United States Trade Representative (USTR), a position created by the Senate Finance Committee, which jealously guarded the jurisdiction of the USTR office and its perquisites. Reagan named to the job Bill Brock, a former senator from Tennessee and Republican National Committee chairman, who enjoyed his own strong friendships in Washington.

Brock and Mac had a good personal relationship, but there was a lot of institutional rivalry between the two entities. The staff at USTR wasted no time in taking anonymous pot shots at Mac and at the Commerce Department in the press. One item appeared in the *National Journal* in March 1981. Citing anonymous sources, the piece reported complaints made by aides to Brock—that there were no advance background papers for the meetings of the new Cabinet Council on Commerce and Trade, and that the session schedule conflicted with two other cabinet-level meetings. Moreover, the sources speculated that this cabinet working group only existed to give Baldrige a role to play; in other words, it was a symbolic "make work" position. Mac ripped out the offensive item, circled it in ink, and sent it to Brock with a handwritten note: "I would admire it if you would stop this kind of crap from the USTR's office as I have from mine. Mac." There is no indication that staff rivalry ended, but he made it clear he would not put up with cheap shots.

Mac had some discretion in how he ran his Department, so he reorganized it to increase the emphasis on international trade. The divisions with expertise in domestic industries (the Bureau of Industrial Economics, the Office of Competitive Assessment, and the Office of Automotive Affairs) were folded into the International Trade Administration (ITA). He wanted the domestic experts to be talking on a regular basis with the international experts to eliminate the lack of coordination between departments that left one arm of

Commerce unaware of the impact of its decisions on the other. It also reflected his view that international trade had a major role to play in the domestic economy. In a shrinking world, the United States needed to sell as many of its goods to as many overseas customers as possible, if the U.S. economy was to recover from and thrive after the oil shock years. In speeches, he said that every billion dollars in exported manufactured goods represented thirty-one thousand jobs. He also reorganized the office of the Chief Economist to upgrade the economic capability of the Department. He combined the Bureau of Economic Affairs, the Bureau of Industrial Economics, and the Bureau of the Census and brought together their statistical and data-collecting ability into a single Policy and Economics Office.

On the economy, the real power center of the government rested with the troika of the Treasury Department, the Council of Economic Advisers, and the Office of Management and Budget. But the Commerce Department was a primary source of high-quality raw data on the gross national product, on housing starts, and other key economic indicators that monitored the state of the economy. These data often influenced the stock market. Good, reliable information is a powerful tool in the hands of someone who understands it and knows how to use it. Mac regularly drew upon the high-level analysis of current and raw data on the U.S. economy.

Reagan took office at a time when the economy languished, and he delivered several major addresses to the nation on economics in his first year in office. During his campaign in 1980, he promoted "supply side" economics, which advocates a reduction in government spending, taxing, and regulation. Opponents called it "trickle down" economics because it presumes that reducing taxes and regulation on the top income earners would eventually "trickle down"

to the less affluent in the form of more jobs and more spending. Supply side economics tended to polarize opinion, even
within the Republican Party. George H. W. Bush had decreed
it "voodoo economics" during his campaign against Reagan,
and Mac is believed to have shared that view. Yet supply
side advocates were convinced that an unfettered economy
kept more money in the pockets of the wealthy and eventually would help everyone else. Reagan won the election, so
the supply siders had tremendous influence in the government. (As a side note, Reagan reportedly became interested
in government and politics when he first began to earn top
dollar as a movie actor. At the time, federal income tax rates
on the highest earners were onerous. President Franklin
D. Roosevelt imposed a 94 percent top income tax rate on
income over $200,000 during the war years. Reagan often
spoke of how he had no incentive to make more than one
movie a year at that time because anything he earned for the
extra work went to taxes. The top rate fell to about 70 percent
in 1964. By 1986, Reagan's second term, the top income tax
bracket rate was 28 percent.)

Mac pushed to make his people, particularly his top
economist, part of the administration's economic forecasting team. While the economist, Robert Dederick, the Under
Secretary of Commerce for Economic Affairs who held a
doctorate in economics from Harvard, says he was often
relegated to second chair by the troika, he was included in
their meetings, and he and Mac became part of the forecasting process. Each time the Department issued new economic
data, which could be a few times in a week, Mac issued a statement on the new data. Often, his analysis was not as sunny as
those favored by the White House press office. For example,
he was the first cabinet official to warn that the fourth quarter
of 1981 and first quarter of 1982 would be difficult, and to
predict that unemployment would rise to more than 9 per-

cent. He quickly acquired a reputation as "good copy" with reporters because of his candor, but more importantly, his predictions proved to be the most accurate. That enhanced his standing with business and the government.

By the end of the first year of the administration, Clyde H. Farnsworth, a highly respected economics reporter for the *New York Times*, wrote that Mac had emerged as the "consensus molder" in the cabinet because he was not identified with any particular philosophical camp, specifically the monetarists and supply siders. The headline of that December article read "Baldrige Sits Tall in the Saddle on Economic Policy" and reported that Mac, a "team player," often expressed the view that it was best to "under promise and over deliver."

STEEL

The Reagan administration inherited a worsening situation on the trade front. For decades, the United States had enjoyed a significant trade surplus. Then abruptly, the situation reversed in the 1970s, powered by America's dependence on foreign oil. By 1983, the trade deficit amounted to $60 billion, eighteen times the 1973 deficit. It was estimated that the trade deficit cost the United States 1.5 million jobs, shrank the industrial base, and sapped economic growth potential. For consumers, it was a mixed blessing. Low-cost goods from overseas were often cheaper and more plentiful than similar items made in the United States, but many Americans also lost the well-paying manufacturing jobs that had boosted them into homeownership and the middle class.

Mac had a keen appreciation of the role that trade played in the domestic economy. Scovill had operated plants all over the world. In a speech he delivered in April 1982 at a Conference on Trade and Investment in Africa, he noted that

U.S. exports increased about five times between 1970 and 1980 to grow to more than 12 percent of the gross national product, almost twice the level of fifteen years earlier. Nearly one-fifth of all goods made in the United States were sold abroad, one of every three acres of farmland produce went overseas, one of every $3 in corporate profits came from international activities, and one of every eight manufacturing jobs depended on exports. The trend was unmistakable; exports would be a key to a prosperous future for America.

He said, "But while the United States is still the most productive and largest economy in the world, we're slipping. In 1960, the U.S. share of world trade in manufactured goods was 25 percent. Last year it was 18.6 percent. It is no coincidence that in the last five years, we've accumulated trade deficits totaling $140 billion." These statistics showed that it was not a decline in U.S. production but the rise of foreign competition that was creating the problems. At the time, the General Agreement on Tariffs and Trade (GATT), a multilateral agreement first adopted after World War II, still governed international trade. Mac was instrumental in launching the Uruguay Round of GATT talks in 1986 to update the agreements. That round resulted in the creation of the World Trade Organization in 1994.

An early trade battle over imported steel was actually a holdover issue from the Carter administration. For years, U.S. steel manufacturers had been complaining about competition from overseas. Mac had a private and less sanguine view of this problem. In his view, the steel company executives had failed to modernize and invest in new equipment and had run their old factories into the ground. He also believed they had failed to keep costs under control.

Thanks to generous union contracts, the typical steelworker made 50 percent more than other industrial workers. Saddled with old furnaces and a gold-plated workforce, the steel companies could barely survive, never mind beat the prices of foreign companies. Even before the recession, the world had excess steelmaking capacity. During the recession, U.S. steel manufacturers were operating at 40 percent capacity. This put a lot of industrial workers on the sidelines. Moreover, the value of the U.S. dollar was inflated, which drew foreign investment to the United States where the dollars could buy more. All of these factors proved to be a deadly combination for the American steel companies. The Carter administration, under pressure from the Steelworkers' Union in the 1980 election year, had raised the protectionist barriers to foreign steel by lowering the price that would trigger tariffs on foreign steel. This caused a spike in the prices of American automobiles, bridges, and railroad cars. The spike benefited the steel companies and their bottom line in the short term but did not address the fundamental underlying problems. Less than a year after the Carter administration concession, the steel manufacturers were back banging their tin cups and demanding more help from the federal government. Seven U.S. steel producers filed antidumping and countervailing duty complaints against foreign manufacturers in eleven countries, including seven in Western Europe. The responsibility for dealing with these cases fell to the Commerce Department, not the USTR, so Mac's trade experts were the people engaged in negotiations to find a more workable solution than the highly punitive, counterproductive tariffs.

Governing is far more complicated than campaigning, where issues tend to be presented as black, white, and absolute. Real life is usually less clear, with multiple shades of gray. While Ronald Reagan could espouse free and open trade during his campaign, as president, he had to balance conflicting constituencies. The Reagan administration's official position favored free and open trade, so government officials could not ignore that platform as a priority. Mac, as a CEO who had sold goods throughout the world, was intimately aware of the benefit of open trade for U.S. businesses. He believed in it. Employment of American workers, however, was also vitally important at a time when unemployment was running high. It fell to Mac to find some sort of accommodation that would head off legislative action from Capitol Hill, where the protectionist sentiment was strong, while maintaining free and open trade in both directions. He feared that extending protection to the U.S. steel industry with a strict new law would trigger a global protectionist war and cause other countries to shut their doors to U.S. goods. These were not unrealistic fears. A few years later, the European community threatened to increase duties on U.S. citrus exports, a huge market for the United States, if the United States reduced imports of steel. To buy some time, Mac launched "investigations" into steelmakers and importers in twelve countries and initiated steel antidumping cases against Japan, Korea, and Yugoslavia. Government investigations and reviews of complaints filed by the industry could take months or years to run their course. The Commerce Department announced that it would review alloy steel imports from West Germany and Austria to determine whether an antidumping investigation was warranted. The administration also engaged in steel talks with European countries in an attempt to forge some sort of agreement to limit imports.

The pressure was intense. The steel CEOs had friends on Capitol Hill and in the administration, and the unions had powerful Democratic friends in Congress where Democrats still held firm control over the House of Representatives. The protectionist sentiment among the unions was very high. They wanted to keep their members on the job. While Mac's investigations and filings were more smoke screen than real change at the time, the flurry of activity appeased the industry and its biggest supporters, and it bought time for the administration as Mac calculated the next steps. Eventually, the Commerce Department negotiated the settlements of dozens of complaints brought by the steel industry. Those agreements effectively set trade policy. His senior staff said that Mac was hands-on in the process of making new trade policies. He held dozens of meetings with European officials and steel company executives. He knew the products, the volume of production, the pricing, and how it all fit together. Just as he learned how to make iron molds, pour iron, and anneal castings at Eastern Malleable Iron Company after the war, he learned every step of the steel business.

Gerry McKiernan, who served as the top congressional liaison at Commerce, remembers one steel deadline with the Europeans that loomed on a Saturday afternoon. An hour before the final negotiation at 10 a.m., Mac called in his team. He told them that an office two doors away from the meeting room had coffee, sandwiches, pastries, and soft drinks. He told them not to let the other side know about the food and beverages. At 12:15 p.m., after more than two hours of discussion, the opposing side suggested a lunch break, but Mac demurred and encouraged them to continue to talk to resolve the issue "because we are so close." At 1 p.m., the American team members began to quietly leave the room one by one for a few minutes, ostensibly to use the restroom. They were actually heading straight to the food room for some sustenance. Finally, at 4 p.m. an agreement was struck. The European side capitulated to the American conditions. "They were starving," said McKiernan. "It was a negotiating ploy."

Mac's position in the cabinet of a president who was unabashedly probusiness, as well as his reputation as a successful industrialist, gave him an excellent soapbox for assessing and criticizing American management practices. He always tended toward candor, but on this topic he was almost brutal in his criticism of his compatriots at the highest levels of

American business. He repeatedly said that too many U.S. business leaders were ignoring business fundamentals, and until they recognized that Japanese and European businessmen were beating them at their own game, all the protectionist steps in the world would not reverse the tide.

In January 1982, he bluntly told the Conference Board in New York City that the Reagan administration was doing what it could to improve the economy and reduce the size and growth of government, but that business had to do its part. "American management has got to question all of its basic principles governing good business practices," he said. "Management is going to have to admit that it's made a lot of mistakes in the past 20 or 30 years. U.S. managers adopted an attitude in the sixties that everything was going well, the quarterly reports were good, so why change anything? Management has got to get away from worrying about short-term returns and start looking at long-term, process-oriented high-risk investments like our foreign competitors. I believe we all have to face the fact that American management productivity has slipped seriously in the last two decades." Mac was saying that our competitors had learned the lessons taught by the United States all too well after World War II and were now beating America at its own game.

The Commerce Secretary's rhetoric grew stronger over time. In a speech in November 1986 he said, "American industries lost ground to foreign competitors because of short-sighted management. We were simply out-managed. Most of all, we lost our reputation for quality when we had been the world's leader. There is no excuse for that and there is no one to blame but American management, not labor, not the government, but management." He cited this compelling example: "We invented the transistor in 1947 and by 1960 we supplied 95 percent of all the radio and television sets sold domestically. Today we don't even manufacture radios and our loss of the color television market is unforgiveable. We pioneered that technology."

In his efforts to find some sort of middle ground between the two extremes on trade, Mac came up with something he called "fair trade." He would say the goal is free trade, but until that existed, we needed to make sure there was "fair trade" among countries. In a speech he delivered at Yale's School of Management in February 1984, he said that free trade was an ideal; government had a responsibility to guarantee fair trade through competitive financing to American companies in certain industries and to impose duties on goods imported from foreign companies that were heavily subsidized by their governments. The purists who opposed any regulation disparaged Mac's comments as protectionism by another name, but there were many significant differences. Trade had been governed by multilateral trade agreements for years. These formal agreements, though, were not very flexible and did not account for unusual circumstances. "Fair trade" was implemented on a case-by-case basis on the flexible principle of reciprocity through the use of diplomacy. It was a far more nuanced approach that required the use of judgment. Mac opposed protectionism in the strictest sense, because it hurt more than it helped. "Protectionism," he said in a speech in 1984, "is a job loser, not a job gainer."

Fair trade was a more targeted and personal approach. Mac led frequent trade missions to make the case in person to foreign heads of state and business leaders. For these missions, he insisted that American corporations send their top people—the CEOs or senior officials capable of making decisions on the spot. He wanted the trade missions to produce results, not just end with a lot of empty promises.

At the same time, he appreciated that foreign countries had their own needs. The U.S. government was not really in the business of picking winners and losers, but in a very real sense, the Reagan administration had to set priorities. The world was changing, so the United States needed to protect its primacy in technology and electronics. If it had to cede a portion of the market for shoes or textiles to the developing nations, so be it. In effect, those industries had been in decline for most of the twentieth century. Of course, it was not as easy as that. The U.S. textile and shoe industries had migrated from the Northeast to the South, where labor costs were lower, earlier in the twentieth century. By the 1980s, developing nations needing to provide employment for their own citizens were promoting manufacturing, particularly in the Pacific Rim. Eventually, many U.S. companies moved their manufacturing factories overseas to take advantage of the lower-cost foreign workers. Powerful lawmakers, particularly southern senators, were looking out for their constituents, so U.S. government officials had to step carefully.

Mac felt that developing nations were ripe for U.S. investment and sales. He saw India and China, then beginning to accelerate their own internal efforts to become more industrialized in a move from rural societies, as prime markets for the United States because of their enormous populations. The International Monetary Fund was investing millions in emerging African countries that were still in the process of shaking off colonialism. These developing nations needed to build modern economies almost from scratch, which created opportunities for U.S. businesses in telecommunications, housing and commercial construction, agriculture and agribusiness. Mac and Agriculture Secretary Jack Block led a trade mission to Cameroon, Ivory Coast, Nigeria, and Morocco early in 1982 that included representatives from twenty-six companies or trade associations. The group included presidents, vice presidents, and CEOs, each of whom paid $10,000 to cover the expenses of the trip. Those on the trip found lucrative business. In Nigeria alone, the successful business deals included large-scale poultry and hog operations, a $100 million dam construction project, an animal feed development project, and a rice-based pasta project. As a result of the trip, the H. J. Heinz Company planned to set up a tomato paste factory in Cameroon, and the Hilton Hotel chain launched a plan to build a hotel in the Ivory Coast.

The steel negotiations with Europe were complicated, lengthy, and difficult. It was not simply a matter of price and the level of imports and exports. The overcapacity of global steel posed a threat to all producers. Unemployment was high in Europe as well, and Mac appreciated the fact that the Europeans wanted to protect those steel jobs as much as Americans did. In the spring of 1982, the talks with the Europeans were teetering on failure during a congressional election year. American off-year elections can be problematic for the president's party. While Reagan had won the presidential election two years earlier, he was now the incumbent, so he was being blamed for the continuing sluggish economy, high interest rates, and high unemployment rate. By August, the Commerce Department under Mac's direction was close to working out a deal with the Europeans, but U.S. steel companies balked because they felt the agreement did not go far enough. Mac called them out on their own shortcomings. He said that U.S. steel productivity problems were hurting the industry far more than unfair trading practices. While he conceded there had been some dumping (foreign exports of steel to the United States at prices lower than their cost to gain an advantage in the market), he considered dumping only part of the problem. "Of course it hurts," said Mac of dumping, "but it's not the determining factor. The determining factor is our ability to compete worldwide."

The steel companies filed dozens of complaints against foreign competitors with the Commerce Department. At one point, there were more than 120 different actions. The

Department had the legal responsibility to investigate these complaints, and Mac saw them as an opportunity to negotiate broader agreements with foreign nations. Besides settling the disputes, these agreements also set policy. In the ongoing power struggle with the U.S. Trade Representative's office, this was considered a win for the Commerce Department, because these agreements had immediate and lasting impact on real sales and conditions.

In October, the European steel industry agreed to cut exports to the United States, and on October 21, just weeks before the November election, Ronald Reagan announced the deal at an event in Omaha, Nebraska. In ten carbon steel product lines in the U.S. market, the Europeans agreed to keep their share to about 5 percent, down from slightly over 6 percent. This kept the European share stable. They also agreed to limit exports of steel pipe and tube to 5.9 percent of the U.S. market, a big drop from the recent 16 percent share. Secretary of State George P. Shultz sent Mac a congratulatory note dated October 22. He wrote, "This has been one of the toughest and most complicated negotiations undertaken by anyone in quite a while, and you have managed—miraculously—to bring it off successfully. You have my admiration, my respect and my thanks." Shultz paid close attention to these trade disputes, because they could and did color U.S. relations with those nations.

This trade agreement proved to be a temporary fix. Brazil failed to keep its end of the bargain, so Commerce had to take action by the spring of 1984. The steel companies still had fundamental management problems, which the LTV Corporation and Republic Steel Corporation tried to resolve by merging. The Reagan antitrust division of the Justice Department objected, citing the antitrust laws approved during the Great Depression.

This time, big steel had Mac on its side. Mac took the macro view of the competitive argument and said that U.S. steel companies needed to be bigger and stronger to compete effectively with foreign players. Mac was relentless, and finally, Paul McGrath, the assistant attorney general in charge of the antitrust division, agreed to give greater weight in future merger cases to the effect imports were having on American industry. This was seen as a major concession by the antitrust division.

In 1984, protectionist sentiment grew even stronger in the United States as former Vice President Walter Mondale, a onetime Minnesota senator who was a great favorite of organized labor, became the Democratic presidential nominee opposing Reagan in his bid for reelection. Mondale favored strict limits on imports, a popular position. The steel executives who were never satisfied by compromises had also stepped up pressure on the administration to get more restrictions on imports.

In what was a surprise to many, in late November the administration imposed an embargo on all imports of steel pipes and tubes from the European community for the rest of 1984 and reduced imports for 1985 to less than half of the European Community's 1984 imports. This was seen as sending a message to the Europeans after months of fruitless negotiations.

The steel negotiations represented the largest trade negotiation during Reagan's first term. The negotiations set the framework for the way the Reagan administration handled trade issues. Establishing quotas on the amount of imports became the preferred approach and a way to avoid countervailing duties in most cases. Countervailing duties on popular foreign goods would raise prices for American consumers and contribute to inflation. The United States also had years of experience with quotas limiting imports of foreign textiles and apparel.

While the steel situation dragged on, there was a growing worry within the Reagan administration over the economic threat posed by Japan. Japanese imports had been steadily increasing over the years. In the 1950s and 1960s, Japanese products were considered substandard, cheap, and disposable. "Made in Japan" was a synonym for tawdry, throwaway junk. That quickly changed as the Japanese began to focus on quality. By 1981, the Japanese were exporting thousands of automobiles and encroaching on the longtime U.S. supremacy in semiconductors. The trade issues with the Japanese became the focal point of Mac's work as Commerce Secretary and a major cause of ongoing concern by the president and his cabinet.

4

JAPAN INC.

America's relationship with Japan was complicated. Japan had been a formidable enemy just thirty-six years earlier. Many titans of industry and top government officials, including Mac, had fought the Japanese in combat. Popular culture, particularly Hollywood movies, portrayed and caricatured the Japanese as hostile and threatening. But as those sharp memories of the war faded and a new generation came of age, the military threat from Japan evolved into an economic threat.

NBC News broadcast an episode of its television show *NBC White Paper* on June 24, 1980, called "If Japan Can . . . Why Can't We?" The show crystallized the economic anxieties of Americans by showing how the Japanese had embraced and implemented W. Edwards Deming's counsel and set up a coherent, well-coordinated, nurtured, continually improving manufacturing system. "That show was a punch to the stomach. It really hit home and said, 'Wow, the U.S. is really in trouble.' This was not just something the policy folks needed to care about. We needed some action by U.S. manufacturers and U.S. government leaders. . . . We could no longer take it for granted that the U.S. was number one," recalled Mat Heyman, who was writing for a technology newsletter at the time and later worked on technology issues at the Commerce Department for many years.

When Japan rebuilt its industrial infrastructure after World War II, the country invested in state-of-the-art manufacturing facilities. The Japanese people accepted a lower standard of living in the short term to make that investment. Japan is a small, homogenous country, an environment in which it is often easier to gain consensus on short-term sacrifices for long-term benefits. While the Allied Occupation systematically took apart the old industrial system of fiefdoms, the system of training and apprenticeships remained centralized. Industry worked closely with the university system, so that university students trained for specific jobs and went into those jobs essentially for their lifetimes. Japanese workers rarely switched firms. As a result, Japanese employees developed a deep loyalty to and understanding of their industries and companies.

Bruce Smart, who served as Mac's second Under Secretary of International Trade, explained, "The Japanese were centrally organized and directed. They had a rather tight network. Mitsubishi would get a group of young people from the University of Tokyo. Those they did not want to keep were sent out to be head of the supplier companies making automobile seats or lighting or some other part. So suppliers were all graduates of the central company culture."

Japan's Ministry of International Trade and Industry (MITI) centralized and molded industrial policy to a degree that U.S. business would likely have found intolerable. Japanese companies were also usually affiliated with a large bank that made access to capital for investment and expansion almost automatic. Japanese firms did not need to go hat in hand to an independent bank to obtain critical financing, and government policy invariably supported industry goals. Japan had developed a virtual monopoly exporting automobiles and other consumer goods to the emerging Asian countries nearby, including Korea, Taiwan, and Malaysia, markets virtually ignored by the United States and Europe. These markets expanded and solidified the sales base of the Japanese market. Japanese goods were considered cheap and shoddy in the first years after World War II, but thirty years later, Japan and its products were a symbol of high quality throughout the world. It was a remarkable turnabout.

Theodore White, the famous journalist and author who brought a historian's eye to his work, wrote an article about the Japanese ascendance that was published in the summer of 1985. "In the 40 years since defeat, Japan has grown to be a giant. Japan has passed the Soviet Union in industrial production and stands as world class No. 2 to our No. 1. If the present Japanese expansion of production continues, it will be, in twenty years, a greater industrial power than the United States. . . . What the Japanese have done since in remodeling the American model is no less than spectacular. They have devised a system of government–industry partnership that is a paradigm for directing a modern industrial state for national purposes . . . and one designed for action in the new world of global commerce that the United States blueprinted." In short, White was saying the Japanese were beating the Americans at their own game.

"Japan was the top trade issue during the first four years of the Reagan administration," said Michael B. Smith, a career foreign service officer who became Deputy U.S. Trade Representative and then acting USTR, after Bill Brock was named Secretary of Labor in 1985. The first Japanese trade problem faced by the Reagan administration involved semi-conductors, essential components in most electronic circuits. The computer industry was beginning to grow exponentially in the United States. Electronic gadgets were becoming more portable and more available to consumers. Transistor radios, for example, were ubiquitous among American teenagers in the 1960s, the iPhone of that era. The first Apple computer, the Apple I, was produced in 1976, and by 1982, *Time* magazine decreed "The Computer" the Machine of the Year in place of its traditional Man of the Year. Computers use memory chips, digital integrated circuits, to store and retrieve data. In 1985, memory chips accounted for 18 percent of all semiconductor purchases in the United States. About 7 percent of this market was made up of dynamic random-access memory chips, or DRAMs, which were quickly becoming a standard commodity used in many different types of electronic devices and computers. In the late 1970s, the Japanese became a major producer of semiconductors, particularly DRAMs. Between 1978 and 1986, the Japanese share of the market jumped from less than 30 percent to about 75 percent, while the U.S. market share plunged from 70 percent to less than 20 percent. Losing dominance on an essential computer component attracted notice from policymakers, who understood its importance for the future. "Something had to be done. . . . We could not have the United States ceding primacy to the Japanese on electronics," said Mike Smith.

The U.S. computer industry reacted with great alarm to this competition and created a trade association, the Semiconductor Industry Association (SIA), to lobby for protection. Government policymakers were uneasy, not just for financial reasons. Electronics were also a key component of defense weaponry and systems, and it was troublesome to be dependent on a foreign country for something so fundamental to national security while the Cold War still raged. While oil and the strong U.S. dollar were driving the burgeoning trade deficit, the goal of energy independence for the United States seemed elusive. Semiconductors were a more manageable challenge. To quantify this threat, the Commerce Department conducted the first broad-based competitive assessment, examining ten primary emerging technologies to measure how the United States stacked up against the Japanese. The investigation concluded that while the United States retained primacy in many of the ten areas, the Japanese were gaining market share, and gaining quickly. Moreover, Japanese government policies were helping Japanese firms, and Americans interpreted the Japanese self-interest as an unfair advantage. The study was widely distributed throughout the administration and on Capitol Hill and had a significant impact on the Reagan administration's trade policy. The assessment resulted in a more robust commitment to demanding reciprocal arrangements with Japan. The United States would keep its doors open to Japan, but Japan had to open its doors to U.S. goods. In other words, the Japanese needed to play by the same rules as the United States. This concept of reciprocity modified the pure free trade approach favored by some in the administration and gradually became the dominant approach of the Reagan administration. The concept of fairness was at the core of this new approach. If everyone followed the same rules, everyone would profit. It was a system intended to make everyone a winner. It also represented a middle ground, a clear compromise between the hard-core free traders and the hard-core protectionists. The ever-pragmatic Mac Baldrige was central to the emergence of this new approach—free and fair trade.

There was considerable foot dragging and resistance from the Japanese to the notion of reciprocity. The Japanese people prided themselves on buying Japanese goods and were not interested in buying American-made products. Their officials complained that the United States was making them a scapegoat, not holding them to the same standard as other nations, and interfering with their own internal affairs to an unacceptable degree. Lionel Olmer, Mac's first Under Secretary of Commerce for International Trade, was on his way to Japan to negotiate a bilateral agreement to set new trade rules on communications with the Japanese early in 1985. Suddenly Mac canceled his trip, announcing that there would be no Japanese trade talks until the Japanese agreed to discuss specific issues rather than broad trade principles, ground that had been covered repeatedly in the past. When AT&T, the giant U.S. monopoly, was broken up to generate a more competitive environment for telecommunications services inside the United States, an unexpected outcome was that Japanese exports to the United States jumped from $600 million to $2 billion a year. The abrupt cancellation of the talks shocked the Japanese and proved to be popular with Americans. It showed the United States was tough. Mac received a personal note from Ralph Regula, a Republican House member from Ohio, which read: "Bully for you!" It was also a very public prod to Japanese officials, who were always cordial but reluctant to roll back what had been great progress for them in the world's markets, particularly in the United States.

Douglas A. Irwin, an economics professor at the University of Chicago who served on the President's Council of Economic Advisers' staff in 1986 and 1987, has written that in addition to Japanese competition, the U.S. semiconductor market faced a lot of problems, such as the high cost of capital, the appreciation of the U.S. dollar, quality control issues, and slow adoption of new processing technology. Not only were Japanese semiconductors better and less expensive but also Japanese companies tended to make everything in-house. They maintained a high degree of vertical integration, as opposed to U.S. companies that purchased components from other manufacturers. The Japanese system in the last half of the twentieth century was called *keiretsu,* a network of inter-locking companies that bought products from one another and excluded other nations' products. It was an effective way to eliminate competition. This also created great efficiency in the Japanese system and reduced overhead costs. Of course, U.S. manufacturers accused the Japanese of "dumping" their products in the United States, selling goods below their manu-facturing costs.

Under American antidumping laws, which Commerce enforced, taxes could be added to the Japanese exports in question, bringing the cost more in line with unsubsidized products. The Japanese did not want high duties on semi-conductors. According to Irwin, U.S. semiconductor manu-facturers wanted some guarantees that the Japanese would not continue to dump semiconductors in third countries, because the lower prices would kill U.S. sales there. Japan eventually capitulated to avoid penalties and sanctions, and MITI put a curb on the quantity of semiconductors exported. This created an enormous windfall for the exporters, which was plowed back into research, development, and product upgrades. Despite its vaunted powers, MITI could not force Japanese companies to buy American semiconductors, so Congress viewed this agreement as a failure and convinced President Reagan to impose 100 percent tariff on $300 mil-lion worth of Japanese imports in April 1987. Irwin says that Japan was stunned by that move, but some MITI officials were secretly pleased, because it proved to Japanese firms that they should follow MITI's directives in the future.

While the semiconductor was important, it was Japanese competition over an American icon, the automobile, which captured the imagination of the public. In 1975, the Japanese share of the American auto market was only 12 percent. Just five years later, in the 1980 election year, it had more than doubled to 27 percent. When U.S. gasoline prices skyrocketed in 1979, American car buyers either stopped buying new cars or looked for smaller, more fuel-efficient imports. The Japanese produced small, energy-efficient cars using the quality control and management techniques learned from Deming. Toyota became famous for operating the most efficient, highest-quality car factories in the world. By contrast, U.S. auto companies were still producing big gas guzzlers—Chevrolets, Cadillacs, Impalas, Buicks, and Oldsmobiles—which had traditionally enjoyed enduring popularity with American consumers. (Lee Iacocca, the famous auto boss, was unusual in recognizing the market for smaller cars earlier than most. He was fired by the Ford Motor Company for his trouble but became legendary as the leader of Chrysler.) With gasoline becoming far more expensive, and memories of gas shortages and long gasoline lines lingering from the 1970s, more and more consumers wanted cars that were less expensive to run. The growth of the American suburbs after World War II meant that workers were commuting significant distances to their jobs every day, so gasoline prices made a big difference in personal pocketbooks. A suburban lifestyle made one, or possibly two, automobiles essential for families. American consumers were voting with their dollars and buying Nissans, Toyotas, and Hondas. The Big Three automakers (General Motors, Ford, and Chrysler) lost $4 billion in 1980 and laid off more than two hundred thousand workers.

While the Japanese could not be faulted for producing popular cars, government policymakers could not ignore the American loss of market share, because the U.S. auto manufacturers represented a huge part of the economy. In addition to auto assembly line jobs, related industries in steel, tires, and many car components comprised a large segment of the U.S. workforce. Automobile dealers proved to be a powerful lobby as well. In those days, auto dealers entered into exclusive contracts with manufacturers to sell specific types of cars. The Chevy, Pontiac, and Cadillac dealers were mainstays in small-town America and were members of the local Rotary Club and Chamber of Commerce, donors to members of Congress, and highly respected community leaders. While plenty of consumers may have wanted to buy inexpensive Japanese cars, most of the political pressure came from the other side to keep imports out and protect domestic manufacturers.

The U.S. auto industry, caught flat-footed, complained to the government and asked for protection from imports. Chrysler had already received a massive bailout from Congress at the end of the Carter administration to keep it from going out of business.

Mac worried that an aggressive protectionist stance could explode into a genuine trade war. To accommodate the Reagan commitment to "free trade" and head off protectionist congressional legislation that Mac was convinced would lead to trade wars, he and other administration officials began urging the Japanese to enter into voluntary restraint agreements (VRAs) at the beginning of the first Reagan term. They hoped that the Japanese would constrain exports without the need for any coercive action from the U.S. government. Lionel Olmer, Commerce's Under Secretary of Trade, said this "voluntary" agreement was a fig leaf to maintain the illusion that the Reagan administration believed the government should not be involved in any restraint of trade. At first, the Japanese paid little attention. They were responding to consumer demand in the United States. They were well aware that high tariffs would cause consumer prices to rise in the United States. But the trade deficit with Japan jumped from $10 billion to $15 billion in 1981, the first year of the Reagan administration; economists predicted it would be up to $20 billion in 1982. At one point, the Reagan administration asked the Japanese government to launch a public campaign to change the ingrained buy-Japanese attitude of Japanese businesses and consumers, a step that would have been laughable had a similar suggestion been made to Americans. After three days of talks in Japan, Mac acknowledged the difficulty in changing the Japanese mind-set. "In recovering after World War II, they grew up with a fierce loyalty to Japanese products," he told reporters. "But now Japan's got to realize that they could be the second largest economy in the world next to us very soon, and when you get to that size, the island mentality isn't big enough." The United States did have inexpensive commodities to sell to the Japanese, particularly in petrochemical feed stocks, beef, and citrus fruits. As the rhetoric escalated and the proposals for strict controls on Japanese imports proliferated in Congress, the Japanese government took notice and became convinced that a voluntary agreement would be better than punitive measures from the most rabid protectionist elements on the Hill.

Mac played an important role in convincing the Japanese to accept this Hobson's choice (an apparently free choice in which there is really only one option). He reached out to the Japanese ambassador to the United States. Joe Wright, the Deputy Secretary of Commerce, who eventually became director of the Office of Management and Budget, remembers Mac asking him to host a dinner at his home for Mac, Midge, the Japanese ambassador to the United States, Yoshio Okawara, and Mrs. Okawara. Mac thought dinner at Joe's house could be conducted without attracting public notice and might offer an opportunity to develop a more personal rapport with the Japanese ambassador.

Ellen Wright, Joe's wife, prepared a simple meatloaf with mashed potatoes and salad. "When we had dinner," said Wright, "Mac insisted on doing the serving. He went right into the kitchen. And afterwards the Ambassador and the Secretary of Commerce were washing the dishes together as they negotiated a trade deal." Ellen did not put up with this long. Concerned they might break something, she shooed them out of her kitchen. While Mac did not really work out the precise terms of an international deal at that dinner, he did help the ambassador understand the U.S. position better and smoothed the way for the voluntary agreements that headed off a real trade war. President Reagan sealed the deal by convincing Japanese prime minister Zenko Suzuki to accept limits on Japanese exports for the stated purpose of giving the U.S. auto industry time to regroup. So in April 1981, the Japanese agreed to put curbs on the numbers of cars they exported to the United States for three years, in what was seen at the time as a victory for the administration. In February 1983, the Japanese extended the limits.

The voluntary agreement, however, did not solve the trade problem. The Japanese gave lip service to increasing American imports. Lengthy debates were held on issues ranging from baseball bats to snow skis to the construction of a new airport in Tokyo. Mac's hope was that if the Japanese increased their purchases of American goods, the trade imbalance would even out, and Americans could still buy those popular little Japanese cars. Moreover, the voluntary restraint did not ease the fervor for more aggressive action from Congress or the manufacturers. By the end of 1982, the administration was feeling more pressure from Congress on Japanese imports. The voluntary agreement may have lowered the rate of increase, but U.S. auto manufacturers were still experiencing fundamental problems and blamed those problems on the Japanese. American auto manufacturers were finally making some small cars, but many consumers saw them as inferior to the high-quality Toyotas and Hondas. A bill to lower imports from Japan and require any foreign automobile manufacturer to assemble their cars in the United States with U.S. parts and labor had passed the U.S. House. Mac went to the Hill to urge the Senate, then under Republican control, to reject it. He succeeded.

A major purpose of the voluntary limits was to give the U.S. auto industry some time to retool so that they might begin to produce the types of smaller, energy-efficient automobiles that American consumers were demanding, and to match Japanese quality. By March 1984, Mac said it was time to drop the Japanese quotas, because the U.S. car manufacturers were healthy enough to compete. The car manufacturers did not agree. Within months, Mac had to reverse himself. It was an election year; Reagan was running for reelection and the Democratic presidential nominee, Walter F. Mondale, was an avid protectionist with strong labor union support. The 1984 trade deficit was running at $130 billion, twice the level of 1983. Voluntary agreements clearly were not doing the trick.

At the same time, changing the traditional way of doing things at auto plants proved difficult, and American consumers had gotten hooked on those small Hondas and Toyotas. Moreover, the Japanese had not given up their preference for Japanese goods. Olin Wethington, Deputy Under Secretary for International Trade, remembers that at a cabinet meeting with President Reagan in December 1983, Mac read a news article that quoted a Japanese business executive as saying that Americans were making their own problems by failing to develop new technologies. The businessman's critique concluded with a politically incorrect assessment, basing America's problem on the fact that Americans had intermarried and "mongrelized" their people, whereas homogeneity was an advantage for the Japanese. The other cabinet secretaries burst into laughter. Reagan hopped from his seat and walked to the exit that took him to the Oval Office. As he left, he turned to his cabinet and said, "Merry Christmas, you mongrels!"

Americans supported free trade in theory, backed protectionist measures to support American industries, and happily bought inexpensive imports. The inherent contradictions of the public view created a constant push and pull between the Reagan administration and Congress throughout Reagan's eight years in office. American executives also displayed a level of arrogance and ignorance of foreign markets. Jim Moore, a deputy assistant secretary of commerce for trade, remembers how executives from the Big Three automakers complained to a Senate committee that the Japanese drove on the "wrong" side of the road and needed to change so that they could drive American automobiles that had a steering wheel on the left. In another case, the CEO of the Smith Corona typewriter company, then based in Syracuse, New York, complained through his congressman that the Japanese were not buying his typewriters. The company, however, was not making a typewriter with kanji characters that the Japanese could use. Requesting federal intervention was a final Hail Mary pass from the typewriter executive because personal computers signaled the death knell for typewriters, and the company ultimately filed for bankruptcy in 1995. "There was a certain American arrogance relative to its own products about getting into the market that was not realistic," said Moore.

The limits on the numbers of Japanese cars only made them more desirable. By July 1983, the voluntary limits had driven up the sticker price of Hondas by thousands of dollars. Americans were not only willing to pay the higher prices, but they were willing to wait months to receive their cars. "It was one problem after the next with Japan. Every time we put out one fire with Japan, there was another," said Moore. The subject of the trade imbalance with Japan came up at least twenty times a year in cabinet meetings, according to Mike Smith, and some meetings turned exclusively on the issue of Japan. Mac was not philosophically opposed to imposing countervailing duties, but he did want to try alternatives first. Then, if those approaches did not work, he would become more aggressive. In April 1987, he was credited in the *New York Times* as the driving force behind the cabinet decision to impose sanctions against Japanese electronics companies in a dispute over computer chips. As a result, 100 percent duties were levied on Japanese color television sets, calculators, power drills, and some computers.

The previous summer, when pricing their semiconductors for the U.S. market, the Japanese had agreed to observe "fair market values" set by the United States. The U.S. government, however, had no way to enforce this agreement and felt it was being undermined by sales of semiconductors to third countries, which would buy the semiconductors at low prices and then resell them to buyers in the United States at a price lower than the fair market value.

Indeed, that March, Mac joined Defense Secretary Caspar Weinberger and the CIA to request that the White House block the sale of Fairchild Semiconductor Corporation, a manufacturer of computer chips and an important defense contractor, to Fujitsu, Ltd. Weinberger and the CIA were primarily motivated by national security concerns; neither wanted the U.S. military dependent upon a Japanese company for critical computer chips. Mac, according to news accounts, viewed the matter as a way to prod the Japanese on the broader issue. While the White House could not easily block the sale, the public objection created such political pressure that the sale was called off within days.

The "problem" of Japan never really went away. Clyde V. Prestowitz Jr., a senior counselor at Commerce during the first Reagan administration, published a book in 1988 titled

Trading Places: How We Allowed Japan to Take the Lead. Japanese companies and individuals later drew attention by buying up some U.S. trophy properties in 1989—Sony bought Columbia Pictures, and Mitsubishi gained a controlling interest in New York City's iconic Rockefeller Center.

Mike Smith says that handling the Japanese trade issue and developing the concept of fair trade were among Mac's greatest legacies. "The Commerce Department did not need any encouragement to go after Japan, but it did need someone at the helm to deal with the hard-liners who wanted to burn Tokyo all over again," he said. Mac was convinced that the dumping issue came back to American management decisions, and if American executives ran their companies well, invested in their people and products, and focused on improving the quality of their products, many of these competitive issues would go away.

Mac was very aware of Japan's Ministry of International Trade and Industry (MITI), which ran the country's industrial policy. In the United States, trade policy was disjointed. The president shared power with Congress and could not easily tell private enterprise what to do. Within the administration, control over trade was deliberately divided between Commerce and the USTR. The Treasury, State, and Defense departments also weighed in on trade issues from foreign policy and national security perspectives.

In the United States, there had been a number of attempts and proposals over the years to centralize control over trade. When Mac went to Japan for three days of talks in May 1983, he could not help but notice how MITI called all the shots. It was easier to deal with a single entity. On that trip, Mac was challenged to arm wrestle a beefy sumo wrestler. The encounter made a classic photo op; the news photographs showed a smiling Mac with the enormous wrestler who wore only the *mawashi*, the traditional belt worn by the wrestlers, covered by a kimono. Mac lost the arm wrestle but convinced MITI to keep the voluntary agreements in place for another year.

It was apparent as early as the Kennedy administration that the State Department, which then held primary responsibility for trade, had different priorities than the business community. Diplomacy and politics would always trump economic and market concerns at the State Department. President Kennedy had created an office of the Special Trade Representative in 1963, taking away some functions from the State Department. That trend continued. Trade reorganization legislation, passed at the very end of the Carter administration in 1980, had divided most responsibility for trade between Commerce and the USTR and continued to draw control away from the departments of State and Treasury. In fact, the legislation shifted State Department employees who worked on commercial trade in consulates and embassies throughout the world to the Commerce Department. This gave Commerce a physical presence overseas, as well as excellent sources of intelligence on economic conditions in dozens of foreign countries. While Commerce benefited from that legal change, Congress had been substantially expanding the responsibilities and power of the U.S. Trade Representative in the 1970s so that the USTR came to be seen as a pet project of the Senate Finance Committee, an extremely powerful legislative panel. When Mac served in the cabinet, the system called for the USTR to set the trade policy while Commerce implemented it.

The trade reorganization legislation adopted at the end of the Carter administration had also given the Commerce Department more power to conduct investigations into dumping. Mac was not eager to levy heavy countervailing duties, because he knew that foreign nations would likely respond in kind. Early in the administration, there was a case brought by the U.S. toy balloon industry complaining about competition from Mexican-made balloons. The new counter-vailing duty responsibility had not yet been fully tested, and this case would set a precedent in the Reagan administration. Mac knew that President Reagan would not want to see a case against Mexico, a neighbor and ally. There was an interagency review of whether Commerce should formally investigate this case, and the top trade officials at Commerce were strongly opposed. Olin Wethington, the deputy undersecretary for trade, remembers staying up all night worrying about it before a crucial cabinet meeting. He met with Mac that morning at eight and recommended that he urge the president to dismiss the case. Mac asked him to accompany him to the cabinet meeting. In the car, Olin handed Mac a fistful of the Mexican toy balloons and suggested they might make a good prop.

"Mac sat one seat over from the president," remembers Wethington. "[Presidential Counselor Ed] Meese started the discussion, and the president just sort of listened. He went around the room and everyone favored taking the case. The only one against it was Baldrige. From the president's body language, you could tell he was uncomfortable accepting a case against his good friends in Mexico. As the discussion was winding down, Baldrige reached into his pocket and pulled out the balloons. The room erupted in laughter. Baldrige said, 'This is what we are talking about.' Reagan said, 'We are going to reject the case.' Baldrige won. Case over."

The top trade experts at Commerce felt strongly that the country would be better off with more centralized control over trade. Olmer and Wethington worked up a proposal to create a new Department of International Trade and Industry (DITI) that would match Japan's MITI. Wethington recalls that Mac found the approach sensible and practical, but he did not want to get into a war with Bill Brock, so he told his experts he would take the proposal to President Reagan if they could convince Brock to support it. After months of

effort, Brock finally signed a letter supporting trade reorganization. Mac briefed President Reagan during a meeting in the
Oval Office and got his support.

Mac invested a lot of personal and political capital in
pushing for a new DITI. Under the proposal, the nontrade
functions at Commerce would be distributed throughout the
government at other departments. Mac, described in news
accounts as the administration's chief salesman for the proposal, was essentially arguing to get rid of his own job and
Department. His aides say, however, that he hoped to be the
new Secretary of International Trade and Industry himself. Not
everyone on the Reagan team liked the idea. The U.S. Trade
Representative staff and the Senate Finance Committee were
particularly opposed. Before Mac briefed the president, he
had convinced Ed Meese, Reagan's powerful counselor, of the
merits of the proposal and, by this time, Mac had solidified his
relationship with the president and his position in the cabinet.

Later that year, Mac and the Professional Rodeo
Cowboys Association sponsored a special Pro Rodeo competition in honor of the president and Mrs. Reagan at the Capital
Centre in nearby Landover, Maryland. The president wore
Wrangler jeans, a leather jacket, a big belt buckle, a cowboy
hat, and a huge smile. President Reagan clearly loved every
second of the competition. He greatly admired the championship belt buckles earned by the victors in the competition,
so Mac arranged for the president to receive a very special
one afterward. At that exhibition, Mac competed in the team
roping event. As his horse chased the steer, Mac swung his
rope over his head, flung it in front of the steer's hind legs
and missed, disqualifying him and his teammate. Because it
was an exhibition, the announcer yelled to the crowd, "Let's
give the Secretary another chance!" Mac declined, saying, "A
cowboy doesn't get a second chance."

In June 1983, President Reagan formally asked Congress to create a new Department of International Trade and Industry (DITI). Bill Brock officially went along with the proposal. The Reagan cabinet was known for its teamwork. A joint statement attributed to Baldrige and Brock gave this rationale for the new agency: "Trade policy formation, negotiation, regulation, and promotion are closely intertwined. . . . We need the institutional strength that comes from combining authority for policy coordination and negotiations with real organizational power and resources. Other major functions in government—foreign affairs, defense matters, financial matters, and others, have strong Cabinet departments responsible for both developing policy and carrying it through to completion. So should trade." With trade deficits growing by the month, the DITI was seen as a way to focus and strengthen the United States' hand in international trade. Senator William Roth, a Republican from Delaware, who years later became best known as the author of the legislation that created the Roth Individual Retirement Account (IRA), had long been a supporter of consolidating the policymaking and implementation functions under one roof. "We need to speak with a single trade voice," he said.

Mac invested a lot of energy and time lobbying for the new DITI. Gerald McKiernan, Commerce's lead congressional liaison, remembers one night Mac had a meeting with a senator at 8 p.m., because it was the only time the senator could spare. As they walked to the meeting in the Russell Senate Office Building, they ran into Senator Barry Goldwater (the Republican from Arizona and 1964 GOP presidential nominee who lost the election to Lyndon B. Johnson). McKiernan remembers, "Goldwater said, 'What the hell are you doing up here? It is eight o'clock at night!' When Mac explained he was lobbying for trade reorganization, Goldwater said, 'I don't know a damn thing about it, but if it means that much to you, I'm for it. Put me in the yes column.'"

From the start, there was resistance to the proposal on Capitol Hill. In fact, with the benefit of hindsight, McKiernan concedes it was probably dead on arrival, given the Senate Finance Committee's determination to guard its prerogatives in the U.S. Trade Representative's office. In addition, other subcommittees in the House and the Senate opposed any structural change that might impinge upon their jurisdictions. While Brock was publicly supportive of the administration's proposal, the senior Commerce staff believes that he quietly worked behind the scenes to scuttle it. McKiernan had worked as a congressional staffer before becoming the Commerce Department's top lobbyist, and he says the proposal collided directly with the deeply entrenched committee system. Certain committees had control over trade policy, and their members and chairmen were disinclined to change anything that might lead to a loss of influence and power.

Even Mac knew the proposal had little chance of success, but he threw himself into it for two reasons: one, he believed in it, and, two, he knew that simply pushing for the new department would get more national attention for trade issues. While important to government officials at the time, trade was not a primary topic among most Americans or American journalists.

In the end, the trade reorganization proposal faced too much opposition on Capitol Hill. This caused a substantial erosion of support internally. At a fateful cabinet meeting, a vote was taken as to whether to continue to press for the proposal. Mac was the only cabinet member in support. After the meeting, Mac told his staff, "I can think of a lot of really *bad* ideas that got more than one vote."

Age ten, 1932—a photo Mac sent "from a regular American boy" to his Uncle Tom Baldrige.

"Yale Buddies' Club," 1942. Front row, left to right: Walter Joseph Patrick Curley, Crawford Greene, Dean Witter. Perched: Malcolm Baldrige, Bob Morton, Martin LeBoutillier. Standing: Hugh Wallace, Abe Hilton.

Captain Malcolm Baldrige, Colonel Howard Malcolm Baldrige, Second Lieutenant Robert Connell Baldrige.

Mac in the army working with his team, c. 1944–1945.

Cedarhurst, Long Island, New York, Summer 1958. From left to right: Mac and Midge Baldrige, Tish Baldrige, Regina Connell Baldrige, Howard Malcolm Baldrige, Robert Connell Baldrige, Nancy Bierwirth Baldrige; children in front row are, from left to right: Alice and Jeannie Baldrige, Molly and Megan Baldrige.

Mac serenades his girls, Megan, age six, and Molly, age four, in 1959. A favorite tune was the classic country song "Letter Edged in Black."

Mac when he was named president of the Eastern Malleable Iron Company, 1960.

Midge and Mac, then president of Scovill Manufacturing Company, at an elegant dinner during a business trip to Brazil, 1962.

Mac relaxing in his customary attire
at the New Mexico ranch, c. 1964.

Official Commerce Department photo,
c. 1981.

Nancy and Ronald Reagan welcome Mac (and Midge, hidden behind him) to a White House dinner held in honor of the nation's governors on February 24, 1981.

Roping practice in Bethany, Connecticut, not far from his home in Woodbury, around 1981.

Secretary of Commerce Malcolm Baldrige visits the nonprofit Pearl Street Community Center in Waterbury, Connecticut, in 1982. Left to right: Pearl Street CC Board Chair Lillian Brown, Commerce Secretary Baldrige, Pearl Street CC Executive Director Hubie Williamson.

Secretary of Labor Ray Donovan makes a presentation to President Reagan and senior government officials and cabinet members. Mac is seated at the table on the right, third from the front, on Reagan's left. This photo was taken in the Cabinet Room at the White House around 1982.

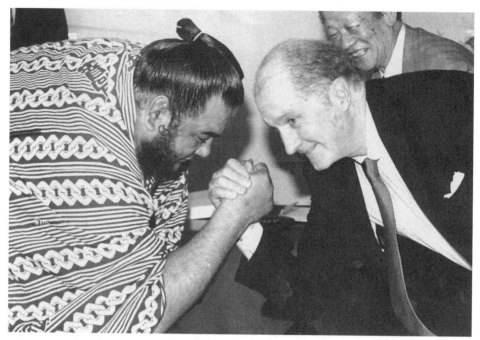

Mac accepted a challenge to arm wrestle sumo champion Jesse Takamiyama on a trip to Japan in 1983. The sumo wrestler won the match, but Mac wrestled some trade concessions from the Japanese government on that trip.

Mac riding in the opening parade at the Professional Rodeo Cowboy Association's exhibition rodeo for President Reagan, in Maryland, 1983.

Mac talks to his boss, President Reagan, on January 12, 1984. They did not know one another well before Mac joined the cabinet, but they quickly became good friends.

After he joined the Reagan cabinet, Mac searched out places to rope in the metropolitan area near Washington, D.C. Here, he practices heeling a steer in Maryland in 1984.

A cabinet meeting, November 13, 1985. Left to right: Secretary of the Interior Don Hodel, Secretary of State George Shultz, President Ronald Reagan, Secretary of Defense Caspar Weinberger, Secretary of Commerce Malcolm Baldrige, Secretary of Transportation Elizabeth Dole.

President Reagan sent this photo taken at the White House to Mac around 1986 with a personal inscription: "Dear Mac—You say you had a loose girth? All the best Mac & Warmest Regard, Ron."

Mac used his bully pulpit at the Commerce Department to expand his influence beyond the limited legal powers of his office. Press conferences like this one were frequent and routine.

Mac works in a hotel room with his longtime chief of staff, Helen Robbins, and his communications director, B. Jay Cooper, during an official trip to Paris in 1987.

Mac grew back the mustache he had in his army days while hospitalized early in 1987. He was still sporting it at an appearance with President Reagan in the spring.

Midge Baldrige's seventy-fifth birthday, August 23, 2002. Left to right: Megan, Midge, and Molly Baldrige.

5

INTERNAL RIVALRIES

IN THOSE FIRST FEW YEARS, MAC HELD HIS OWN IN THE interagency rivalries of the Reagan administration. This was viewed as surprising given the inherent limitations of the powers of his office. A great deal of credit for his success is given to his personality; his personal relationships with the president, vice president, and other cabinet officials; and his forthright, practical approach. He believed in making things work and getting things done. According to many of his contemporaries, President Reagan listened to Mac and respected his advice. Mac "was a pragmatist," said William Archey, the Acting Assistant Secretary for Trade Administration. "He was a very likable guy and a practical guy. Mac used to be set up by the White House to put fires out because he was well liked, respected, and a straight shooter. At one point in time, he was the only Cabinet officer welcomed on the Hill. People on the Hill from both parties liked him."

Mac's candor and command of the facts proved to be invaluable, but he was not always able to persuade the president, despite the credibility he earned by being the first senior adviser to warn President Reagan that a deep recession was unfolding during the summer of 1981. Nearly a year later, in the spring of 1982, the economy was still lagging. President Reagan had made campaign promises to reduce taxes and increase defense spending, but the government was running a serious budget deficit in excess of $100 billion. The business community wanted the deficit reduced, and Mac recommended that the president adjust his plans and take steps to reduce government spending by another $20 to $30 billion. But the president insisted on sticking with his program. After leaving the West Wing, Mac told his staff "I broke my pick" in a vain attempt to persuade the president to modify his program and limit the growth of red ink. He often spoke of his admiration for Reagan's steely determination and his "cast iron" backbone. Yet from all indications, President Reagan appreciated Mac's candor. It is easy for a president to become isolated from reality. Then, as now, few are willing to speak the truth to those in power, but successful leaders invariably surround themselves with people who will be honest with them.

While Mac had a defined and clear point of view, he was not rigid, and this was an element of his success. Mac's position on economic issues was not necessarily predictable. He tended to take a case-by-case approach. In general, however, he saw his role as the advocate for American business, and he argued the business case for more trade and reduced barriers to exports. He was forthright in his advocacy and pulled few punches for political reasons. For example, he was willing to needle longtime ally Canada for subsidizing the production of subway cars, which hurt U.S. manufacturers. But true to his free trade instincts, Mac opposed placing countervailing duties on imported Canadian softwood lumber. Canadian officials were grateful for this nuanced position. He received personal notes from high-ranking Canadian officials thanking him profusely for opposing the high tariffs.

The Reagan cabinet was a collection of peers. As Tom Collamore, a longtime top aide to Mac, noted, the cabinet members were "adults" who generally respected one another, engaged as equals, and disagreed, usually without being disagreeable. Of course, there were always hot heads. Alexander Haig, the onetime military general and Reagan's first secretary of state, was known to raise his voice and pound the table to make a point. Those who witnessed these outbursts remember that Mac often stepped in as the cool, even-handed, genial cabinet member who thanked Haig for his comments, smoothed over the awkwardness, and helped move the meeting along to the next subject.

Since that time, White House staff members have become more powerful, and presidents now tend to govern through their senior staff, rather than their cabinet. To some degree, this was beginning to take place as the Reagan administration matured. All presidents seem to consolidate power in the White House, but the basic dynamic of the cabinet government approach still remained the same. For example, a Reagan White House staff member would not likely call a cabinet official on the carpet, although Reagan's staffer might call to let the cabinet member know of a problem or concern. The difference in tone is a crucial distinction.

"Mac worked those relationships [on the Cabinet]," said Collamore. "He understood the importance of those personal relationships." Even though Mac grumbled about the constant socializing, particularly the black tie events, both he and Midge recognized and accepted the value of those social relationships in Washington where cocktails, dinner parties, and charitable galas greased the skids of government. It was not unusual for a cabinet secretary, a U.S. senator, and a top columnist to be seated together at a dinner in a Georgetown mansion. It was difficult, if not impossible, to demonize someone who talked to you at length about his children at dinner the night before. Midge and Mac got to know senior White House staff, other cabinet members, and members of Congress, including those from the Democratic Party, during those social engagements. Already sharing a social relationship turned any discussion of policy differences into a far more amiable exercise.

In January 1986, Mac sent a dress shirt with snaps instead of buttons and studs to each member of the cabinet. He wrote the same note to each: "Dress shirts take too much time. My old company has a division making snap fasteners for western shirts, so I asked them to put them on a dress shirt three years ago. That shirt has saved me a lot of time and aggravation. With no cufflinks or studs to fool around with, you can clearly put it on in a hurry. And sometimes you may want to take it off in a hurry." The gift was accepted with delight and considerable amusement over the speculative mention of taking the shirt off quickly. In a typical handwritten thank-you note, Bill Brock, then the Labor Secretary, wrote, "Quick draw Baldrige does it again! Super idea and great present . . . thanks a million, Bill." Peers viewed Mac and Midge as a lot of fun. Mac dressed up as Santa Claus for a Christmas party sponsored by Roy Pfautch and held at the Marriott Hotel in downtown Washington in December 1986. As Santa, he presented a special birthday cake to Ed Meese, who by then was serving as the attorney general. In another sign of those times, Pfautch's party was a sought-after ticket (entry required the guest bring a toy for a needy child) and was bipartisan.

While the differences of opinion and rivalries over policy inside the Reagan White House rarely became personal, they were significant. President Reagan was serious about reducing the size of government, and his feisty budget director, David Stockman, slashed and burned his way through the bureaucracy with sweeping proposals that eliminated jobs, programs, and sometimes entire agencies. While some of the reductions were likely warranted, Mac spent a lot of time fighting off proposals he considered ill advised or counterproductive. Kay Bulow, an Assistant Secretary of Commerce, remembers Rep. Neal E. Smith, a longtime Democrat from Iowa who held the chairmanship of a key House Appropriations Subcommittee, asking Mac how he would balance the trade deficit with Japan. Mac replied, "Trade one hundred Japanese engineers for ten thousand of our lawyers." Technology exports were growing in importance as the industry itself developed and matured. Mac streamlined the approval process for technology export licenses as part of his overall effort to improve the operation of the enormous Commerce Department bureaucracy. In 1982, the U.S. government approved $500 million worth of licenses to export technology. In 1983 the Commerce Department processed 140,000 export licenses. During the first four months of 1985, the government was approving licenses at a rate that would amount to $3 billion for the year. This huge increase reflected the growing value and importance of technology as an export product for the United States.

This did not always sit well with his colleagues. With the Cold War against the Soviet Union still dominating U.S. foreign policy, the Secretary of State, the Treasury Secretary, and Secretary of Defense often objected to Mac's intent to increase trade with the USSR or make available for sale overseas items that were even remotely high-tech. The other secretaries worried that these products might be used in defense weaponry and systems that could somehow get to the Soviets. Mac was as patriotic as the next cabinet member, but he was convinced that more could be done on the economic and trade side without harming U.S. security, and he believed that deeper economic relationships with the West would eventually modify behavior on the security and diplomatic fronts. This proved to be true. History shows that trade has often been the first and primary way distant countries interact in any meaningful way. In the decades after Mac's death, trade of products expanded into services, intellectual property, and communications. Improvements in communications, particularly the widespread availability of television, satellite, and the Internet, brought rapid change to once remote, isolated places, helping fuel indigenous nationalist and anticommunist movements.

The day after Christmas in 1991, four years after Mac's death and nearly three years after Reagan left office, the Soviet Union was formally dissolved. The remaining twelve member republics became independent. It was a stunning and quick end to the rivalry between the USSR and the United States, which had dominated international policy for almost fifty years since World War II. While hindsight suggests that the Reagan administration's hard-line posture probably put the final bit of pressure on the Soviet Union's weak system and contributed to its collapse, there were few signs of the imminent collapse during the Reagan years. With no crystal balls in the Cabinet Room during Reagan's presidency, the arguments were fierce against exports of the so-called dual-use technologies that might have defense applications.

There were fundamental disagreements between what the Defense Department officials viewed as national security interests and Mac's view that these prohibitions were excessively cautious and prevented an American growth industry from selling products abroad. The Treasury Department's Customs Department objected to seemingly innocuous items as "threats" to U.S. security. Years later, one senior Commerce Department official acidly complained that the Customs

Department would object to the trade of chopsticks as a threat to national security. Defense Secretary Weinberger opposed any engagement with Russia and went directly to the National Security Council to object to Mac's plans to travel to Moscow on a trade mission in 1985. The trip was the first high-level meeting on U.S.-Soviet trade since 1978. The Soviet invasion of Afghanistan in 1979 effectively ended most high-level contacts between the two countries. In 1984, U.S. exports to the Soviet Union amounted to $3.2 billion; all but $470 million consisted of shipments of grain and other agricultural products. Mac was scheduled to meet with the Soviet Minister for Foreign Trade, Nikolai S. Patolichev, to discuss the sale of nonstrategic advanced oil drilling technology.

Weinberger strongly opposed the contact. He felt it was a mistake to sell technology of any type to the Soviets, and he wanted to protest what he viewed as Moscow's cavalier attitude regarding the killing of an American army major by a Soviet sentry near a Soviet installation in East Germany early that spring. Weinberger felt so strongly that he made a personal appeal to President Reagan after he failed to convince the NSC to call off the trip. Reagan sided with Mac. He wanted the high-level contacts to take place.

Bill Archey, in Commerce's Trade Department, was at the center of many of these "dual-use" conflicts and is convinced that some of the pressure from the Defense Department was little more than a power play. The Defense Department officials wanted to have the authority to regulate exports and not merely be an agency allowed to "review" decisions made by the Commerce Department. He remembers one incident involving a New York company that wanted to sell a high-tech fiber overseas. Fully aware that the technology had many applications, including defense applications, the Commerce Department reviewed the sale very carefully before approving it, with many conditions. Defense Secretary

Weinberger complained to Mac that Archey was not allowing the Defense Department to review the license application. Mac called Archey in to discuss it. "So, Mac said, 'Has he got a case?'" recalled Archey. "I said, 'No, this is the best job we have ever done on a national security case and we put all kinds of conditions on it.'"

When Mac asked him what he thought they should do about Weinberger, Archey replied with an expletive. "I said, "Frankly, Mac, [#@!&] them!" with a blunt obscenity. Mac looked at him evenly and nodded in agreement. "You are right," he said. Archey knew his boss well and anticipated his response. He promptly handed Mac the letter he had already written for him to send to Weinberger explaining the decision. Mac signed it and sent it to the Defense Department, which never replied but backed off the argument.

In a counterintuitive move that likely helped him make his case, Mac made a very public fuss early that year over the fact that military and technical secrets were slipping into Soviet hands. He said that the Department of Defense was not checking documents for strategic information before automatically declassifying and making them available to the public. The Soviets snapped up every technical study as it became available, and plumbed each for information they could use. While this is an inevitable downside of an open society with government records that are public information, Mac viewed this as a backdoor intellectual drain that was more damaging to U.S. security than the sales of agricultural or drilling equipment.

In these internal battles between commercial and security concerns, Richard N. Perle, an assistant secretary of defense who had built a long and formidable career as a hard-line Cold Warrior, ranked among Commerce's most prominent rivals. Perle was well on his way to becoming a singular policy force; he was effective, and he played hardball.

International Harvester, a major U.S. manufacturer of farm and construction equipment, was financially weak. Consolidation of American agriculture into agribusinesses had reduced demand for equipment. In 1980, the company sold twenty thousand agricultural combines to the Soviets. In 1981, the company wanted to sell the Soviets the blueprints and knowledge to construct a factory in the Soviet Union capable of producing thirty thousand grain harvesters each year. There was a precedent for trade related to agriculture, largely for humanitarian reasons. The USSR had a history of bad harvests, and the United States had agreed to sell to the Soviets eight million tons of grain each year in a 1975 trade agreement negotiated during the Ford administration. Even earlier, President Nixon had negotiated a wheat deal with the Soviets, the first trade agreement to include a human rights component (requiring the Soviets to allow the emigration of Soviet Jews). In January 1980, President Jimmy Carter, facing a difficult campaign for reelection, imposed an embargo on sales in excess of the eight million tons allowed in the 1975 agreement. The grain embargo reversed his pledge to Iowa farmers made four years earlier and was grievously unpopular with farmers who had enjoyed a robust harvest in 1979. The embargo was a way to make Carter appear tougher in foreign policy.

The Defense Department opposed the International Harvester deal, and Richard Perle led the charge, even leaking the story to columnist George Will, stating that the United States was selling out to the communists. In a widely distributed newspaper column published in October 1981, Will all but called the Commerce Department officials traitors and collaborators. (Perle and Will had been like-minded classmates in graduate school at Princeton's political science department.) Mac was far from a voice in the wilderness advocating the sale; he had some powerful support. Senator

Charles Percy, a Republican from Illinois, the home state of International Harvester, wanted the sale to succeed to help the company stay afloat and keep its workers and his constituents employed. The Commerce Department staff quarterbacked an interagency investigation into the merits of the Defense Department's objections and systematically shot down or disproved each objection in a painstaking review. Six months later, the sale went through. These victories all required a heavy investment of time and effort and were frequently achieved only after tedious negotiations.

Mac discovered the existence of an obscure entity called the Export Administration Review Board, which proved to be a useful tool to speed up approvals and resolve differences between departments. The Board was created by the Export Administration Act of 1979 and consisted of some of the most powerful officials in Washington, including the secretaries of Defense, State, Treasury, and Energy, as well as the director of the Central Intelligence Agency and the president's National Security Council adviser. The purpose of the board was to consider export controls on sensitive dual-use goods and technologies. The Bureau of Industry and Security at the Department of Commerce administered it. The federal government is full of these sorts of obscure commissions and boards, and they frequently languish, inactive and forgotten, for years.

Once Mac learned of the existence of this board, he decided to use it to press for more exports. The law required board members to attend meetings held at the Commerce Department and chaired by Mac. Until then, it was unheard of for the secretaries of State, Treasury, and Defense, the three most powerful members of the cabinet, to go to the Commerce Department for a meeting. Each outranked the Commerce Secretary, and protocol required the Commerce Secretary to go to their offices to meet. But they all went to

Mac's office. Sitting together around a conference table, these officials discussed and worked out many differences. The deputies, including Richard Perle, were cut out of the process, because the law specifically required the principals to meet, discuss, and resolve the issues. Mac used those meetings to get a fairer hearing on many export issues.

In July 1984, the *New York Times* reported on a turf battle between Mac, Defense Secretary Weinberger, and Customs Commissioner William von Raab. With Mac managing to persuade President Reagan to overrule some national security concerns and allow trade, his rivals quietly convinced friends on Capitol Hill to file legislation that would remove export control authority from the Commerce Department and give it to the Customs Department, a division of Treasury. In the midst of this battle, Mac and Midge received a gracious note from Ed Meese dated July 14, 1984, thanking them for hosting him at a dinner at their home. Meese proved to be an important ally for Mac in the West Wing.

Mac did not win every battle. In some cases, foreign policy concerns trumped economic considerations. For example, President Reagan broadened restrictions on the export of equipment for the planned $10 billion Siberia-to-Europe natural gas pipeline in June 1982. The ban was in response to the harsh martial law imposed by the authoritarian military regime in Poland (with Russia's encouragement and blessing) that banned prodemocracy movements and severely restricted the personal freedom of Polish citizens. The ban on high-technology oil and natural gas equipment to the Russians was strongly opposed by European allies. Europe needed a ready source of natural gas, and Siberia had an ample supply. The pipeline would expedite the delivery of oil and gas to European customers. The European anger over the pipeline ban complicated Mac's efforts to resolve the steel issue. Reagan made the announcement while Mac was in Brussels for talks with the Europeans over steel. A senior U.S. official told the *Wall Street Journal*, "All they wanted to do was talk about the pipeline. You read a lot about European resentment of the pipeline decision, but you have to see it to appreciate it."

The following year, Mac was able to modify that ban to allow Caterpillar Tractor to sell to Russia special heavy-duty tractors used to lay enormous pipes in the trenches of the pipeline. The ban had cost Caterpillar, then suffering from financial difficulties, about $90 million in sales. The president agreed to allow the sale over the strong opposition of the Defense Department after he was convinced there were no military applications for the tractors.

In early spring 1982, the Ionics Company, a Watertown, Massachusetts, manufacturer of water purification equipment, tried to ship almost a million dollars of equipment and chemicals to Libya, in advance of an embargo deadline imposed by the U.S. government to punish Libya for its support of terrorist groups. Customs agents seized six containers of Ionics goods headed for Libya at the Brooklyn, New York, waterfront. After complaints from the company and the company's local congressman, House Speaker Thomas P. "Tip" O'Neill Jr., the Commerce Department managed to get two of the shipping containers freed for export on a technicality. These sorts of cases, where the Commerce Department lobbied internally for a U.S. company, became routine.

In some national security issues, Mac shared the more hard-line approach. In 1974, the Jackson-Vanik Amendment denied Most Favored Nation status to any country that restricted the emigration of its own citizens. Richard Perle helped draft that amendment when he worked for Senator Scoop Jackson, who was strongly anticommunist. The Reagan administration adopted a quiet internal policy that high-level meetings with a Soviet official include a request to release a

Jewish *refusenik*, one of the Soviet Jews agitating for the right
to leave the Soviet Union, where Jews faced significant dis-
crimination and were not free to practice their religion. The
issue of emigration came up at the first meeting Mac had with
his Soviet counterpart in May 1985.

A classified cable sent back to Washington reveals that Mac
did not engage in diplomatic niceties when he spoke to Foreign
Trade Minister Patolichev. The telegram said: "In a sometimes
tense and confrontational meeting, Secretary Baldrige and
Minister Patolichev disagreed over Soviet emigration and the
question of sending letters to the respective business commu-
nities to urge them to do more business with each other. . . .
Secretary Baldrige tersely told Patolichev that he could not in
good faith urge U.S. companies to increase efforts to sell in
the Soviet Union after a seven-year hiatus unless the Soviet side
indicated a willingness to do business with U.S. firms. Looking
extremely serious, Baldrige said that if Patolichev were not
willing to do that, we had come halfway around the world for
nothing. There was little point in going ahead." The Soviet officials huddled to discuss what amounted to an ultimatum, and
Patolichev agreed to send the letter.

The Soviet Union wanted Most Favored Nation status in
trade, the classification reserved for friends and allies, but it was
expressly forbidden by the Jackson-Vanik Amendment as long
as the Soviet government imposed restrictions on the movement of its own citizens. Mac pulled out a copy of a letter to
Patolichev signed by 116 members of Congress insisting upon
a change in policy on emigration. He told the Trade Minister
that there would be no meeting and no trade agreement unless
there was a policy change, because only Congress, the men and
women who signed that letter, could change the law.

Mac was the first American government official to meet
with Mikhail Gorbachev shortly after his election as General
Secretary of the Communist Party in March 1985. At the age

of fifty-four, Gorbachev was the youngest member of the Politburo, the first Soviet leader born after the Communist Revolution, and a man with a mission to reform the Soviet system. The Soviet economy was in shambles, and he became convinced that social and political reforms were required as well. While his goal was to maintain the centralized system of the USSR, his policies of *glasnost* (openness) and *perestroika* (restructuring) inadvertently contributed to the eventual collapse of the Soviet Union in 1991. Mac recognized an opportunity for the United States in Gorbachev's approach. In fact, he agreed to lift a thirty-four-year ban on the sale of Soviet fur skins, which had long been sought by American furriers who said that the Soviet skins ended up in the United States as finished products anyway.

They met for more than two hours. Gorbachev wanted Most Favored Nation status and said that trade could help "defrost" relations between the two countries. Mac brought with him a letter to Gorbachev from President Reagan, which expressed in general terms the wish for expanded trade between the two countries. They talked about horses and exchanged pleasantries. Mac later told reporters that he was impressed that Gorbachev was a youthful and intelligent leader, a true professional, who genuinely wanted a new beginning in his country's relationship with the United States. Both men saw trade as a way to bridge some of the long-standing differences. The meeting was largely atmospheric and cosmetic in policy, but it was an important part of an ongoing process that gradually improved the tense relationship between the two superpowers. Mac delivered a firsthand report to President Reagan and the other cabinet officials when he returned to Washington. Staff members in attendance say that the report was delivered to a rapt audience in the Cabinet Room.

To be sure, the relationship between the United States and the Soviet Union was far from friendly and warm. The Russians were aware of Mac's cowboy background, so his hosts had scheduled a trip to a farm outside of Moscow that bred fine horses worth a million dollars each. After parading out several to show to Mac and his party, the Russians, who knew Mac was a skilled rider, offered him the chance to ride one. Mac mounted the horse and rode it around the arena. When he dismounted, he went over to an aide and said, "That was the rankest horse I ever rode." "Rank," in rodeo-speak, means it was a mean, difficult horse to ride. Mac told the aide that he believed the Russians deliberately offered him an uncooperative horse so he would be bucked off and embarrassed. Midge then mounted the same horse and she, too, being an experienced horsewoman, rode the horse without incident. Then the wife of the ambassador to Russia climbed aboard. She was not as experienced a rider, and she was promptly thrown. Midge also reports that at this foray, Russian photographers were snapping shots with a strange camera, mostly of Mac's hands. There was speculation among the U.S. contingent that it might have been a way for the Russians to determine the status of Mac's health.

The trade mission produced modest results. Later in the year, U.S. companies reported a significant difference in their treatment by Moscow. They told U.S. officials that it was easier to make appointments with Soviet officials, and those officials now seemed more interested in dealing with them. The estimate was that there had been about $60 million in new U.S. sales to the Soviet Union since the meetings Mac held in Moscow the previous spring. It was not a lot of money, and even Mac said that U.S.-Soviet trade was likely to remain a very small portion of overall trade for the United States, but a foot was in the door. In many cases, Mac simply wanted U.S.

firms to be able to compete for the business that U.S. allies were enjoying in the Soviet bloc countries. His feeling was that if the communist countries were going to buy goods and services from foreign sources anyway, they might as well get them from Americans.

There is no indication that any of Mac's colleagues felt any personal hostility toward him when he opposed them on policy issues. Indeed, he received personal notes congratulating him on trade achievements from Secretary of State George Shultz and others. His personal style, his steady demeanor, and his ability to make other cabinet officials feel respected and noted served him well. "Mac was the guy who was turned to when factions got noisy in cabinet meetings. Mac would calm things down," said Michael B. Smith, a deputy USTR who attended dozens of those cabinet meetings. An Under Secretary for Economic Affairs at the State Department, W. Allen Wallis, who was best known as the president of the University of Rochester, was seventy years old in 1982 and something of a curmudgeon. He was such a strong advocate of free trade that he had no concern for the effects on U.S. industries or their employees. Even Wallis liked Mac, who managed to persuade him to support Mac's position on the semiconductor issue with the Japanese.

Mac showed no reluctance to use a national security argument if it would protect a U.S. industry. No one in the cabinet, including Mac, wanted the United States to be dependent upon a foreign nation for production of a major weapons system or the components that made up jet planes, submarines, or aircraft carriers. The decline in manufacturing in the United States had generated a great deal of concern about maintaining enough of an industrial base to avoid that type of dependence in the military arena. In fact, members of Congress entered into compromises to subsidize and share construction contracts for critical military hardware. For example, the Mississippi and Maine delegations split the work for construction of navy destroyers for years. While those destroyers could likely have been built for less money overseas, it was seen as critical for U.S. security to retain the domestic ability to build destroyers in the event of a national emergency, even if the government had to pay a premium to do so by maintaining two shipyards hundreds of miles away from one another. Redundancy was built into this policy; in the event an enemy attack disabled or destroyed one shipyard or manufacturing complex, the other could continue to produce the destroyers or whatever else was needed for defense. Mac used the national security argument to recommend sharp limits on the importation of machine tools to protect the domestic industry. His proposal banned 90 percent of all imports and effectively eliminated most Japanese machine tools from the U.S. market in March 1984.

For all his efforts, the trade deficit kept worsening. For example, each quarter of 1984 set a new record for the trade imbalance. In 1985, the first year of his second term, President Reagan created a Trade Strike Force chaired by Baldrige that included the secretaries of Treasury, State, Transportation, and Agriculture, along with the U.S. trade representative. The purpose was to identify barriers to U.S. exports and unfair subsidies used by foreign governments to promote the sales of their products in the United States. The Strike Force was a response to a trade bill then being debated in the Senate, which would have reduced textile imports from a dozen countries, most of them in Asia. The Commerce Department opposed this rollback. The Strike Force proved to be so much window dressing that months later it was deemed a failure by the *Wall Street Journal.*

While Mac won more of these internal battles than he lost, he was careful not to lord his successes over his colleagues and scrupulous in keeping any difference of opinion from turning into a personal grudge. Joe Wright remembers the time that David Stockman, the budget director, opposed a proposal to put up a second weather satellite for NOAA. One of the two costly weather satellites, which monitored atmospheric conditions and provided the information needed to forecast the weather, was beginning to lose power, and there was a dire need to replace it. Stockman, responsible for reducing government spending, suggested that the Commerce Department let its sole healthy satellite drift into a spot over the middle of the country and monitor the weather on both coasts. Mac had the staff put together a presentation for him to take to the president.

According to Joe Wright, Mac showed a satellite photograph of the continental United States to President Reagan and asked, "Mr. President, do you believe that Hawaii is part of the United States?" The president replied, "Well, of course, Mac." And Mac continued, "Do you notice that Hawaii is not on the chart with Dave's idea?" That ended the matter. The president was convinced, Stockman was overruled, and Commerce got its second satellite.

Senior Commerce Department staff remember that Mac viewed Stockman as a bit of a bully. Stockman, a former member of Congress, was young and somewhat brash. He had a reputation as precocious, pugnacious, and effective. But Mac did not let the policy differences get in the way of a cordial personal relationship. A two-day snowstorm in February 1983 left Washington buried in the second highest snowfall ever recorded in the city and threatened to disrupt Stockman's wedding to Jennifer Blei at the Hay-Adams Hotel just a block from the White House. Mac and Midge loaned the couple their four-wheel-drive Jeep. Stockman and his bride wrote them a note afterward expressing "our lasting appreciation for coming to our rescue with the four-wheel drive on our wedding day." They wrote that the vehicle shuttled parents, bridesmaids, and ushers throughout the day and even took the preacher home after the ceremony. They wrote, "All have a renewed faith in the Reagan administration: if the Secretary of Commerce can't control the weather department at least he provides a pretty impressive and reliable 'safety net.'" When Stockman resigned in 1985, Mac turned down the offer to replace him, preferring to stay with the trade issues at Commerce.

His rapport with his colleagues sometimes allowed him to forge unusual alliances on specific issues. Secretary of State George Shultz and Treasury Secretary James A. Baker sided with Mac in May 1985 on the position that contracts already signed by American importers and exporters should be exempt from the economic sanctions then going into effect against Nicaragua. Cap Weinberger and Robert ("Bud") McFarland, the National Security Council adviser, were opposed. Mac's side won. Mac often worked with Agriculture Secretary Jack Block, whose wife, Sue, became a good friend of Midge. Block, a highly successful Illinois farmer, wanted Reagan to lift Jimmy Carter's grain embargo against the Soviet Union. Alexander Haig, then the Secretary of State, and Defense Secretary Weinberger were on the other side. Mac and Bill Brock agreed with Block, and recruited to their side two of the president's most powerful staff members, Ed Meese and Chief of Staff Jim Baker. Meese and Baker, both veterans of the Reagan campaigns, appreciated the political importance of the sale to American farmers. Reagan lifted the embargo in April 1981.

There were some internal battles that were almost comical. U.S. Rep. Virginia Smith, a Republican from Nebraska and longtime member of the House Appropriations Committee, was greatly concerned that President Reagan's budget proposal for 1983 would shut down a one-person weather station in Valentine, Nebraska, which served the

Sandy Hills section of her district. About seventy-five volunteers watched the weather in their areas and reported regularly to the sole employee. The budget proposal prepared by David Stockman's staff at OMB called for the elimination of a group of weather stations: twenty-five full-time, twenty part-time, seven agricultural, and five fire-related stations, including the one in Valentine. Congresswoman Smith, then in her seventies, had a very high-pitched voice. When it was her turn to question Mac, who was the witness before the committee that day, she spoke at length about the importance of the Valentine, Nebraska, weather station. Mac said he had not been to Valentine in a very long time, but he was certain he had spent a night in jail there after he and a few friends busted up a local bar. He promised her the people of her congressional district would continue to get weather coverage. Mac spent a great deal of time accommodating these types of requests, because he understood that saving a one-person weather station in Valentine, Nebraska, translated into political capital that he could use on more important issues.

Mac enjoyed good relationships with members of Congress, including Democrats, who warmed to his no-nonsense demeanor and appreciated his straightforward style. He was viewed as a man of his word, which counts for a great deal in the corridors of power. The Department's chief lobbyist, Gerald McKiernan, said that members of Congress often supported Mac because they liked him. McKiernan says that the Reagan administration's modest trade agenda in the first term secured approval from Congress because Mac was able to persuade key chairmen, including representatives Ferdinand St. Germain, a Rhode Island Democrat, and Peter Rodino, a New Jersey Democrat, of the merits of the proposals.

Mac never "went Washington" as some high-ranking officials do, but he did relish parts of the Washington scene.

McKiernan remembers attending a midmorning meeting with Mac and Senator Jack Danforth, a Republican from Missouri, at Danforth's office in the Russell Senate Office Building. Suddenly, the senator's secretary interrupted to say that Mac was needed at the White House immediately for an emergency cabinet meeting. They rushed to the car. Gerry claims that Wesley Goad, the Secretary's driver, had the car moving before the doors closed. Wes put his flashing light on top of the red Mercury and sped down Pennsylvania Avenue, ignoring red lights, to get his boss to the White House. The car had two car phones. (This was long before cellular smartphones.) One rang and it was Craig Fuller, the White House secretary for the cabinet, briefing Mac on the reason for the meeting. Then the second phone rang. It was Ed Meese lobbying Mac to support his view on a policy point at the upcoming meeting. As they turned into the White House grounds, the Secret Service uniformed guards recognized the Secretary's car, the distinctive red Mercury sedan, and opened the gate. The car pulled up to the White House and Mac turned to Gerry, a Connecticut native, and said, "Beats the hell out of Waterbury."

6

THE SECOND TERM

PRESIDENT REAGAN WON REELECTION FOR A SECOND TERM in a landslide victory over former Vice President Walter F. "Fritz" Mondale on November 6, 1984. He carried forty-nine of the fifty states. Mondale carried the District of Columbia and barely squeaked through in his home state of Minnesota. A reporter asked Mac if he felt burned out after four years in Washington. Mac enthusiastically responded: "Hell no. I'm just getting warmed up!" In fact, Mac's impact on policy would crest and culminate in the second term.

The dynamic of a second presidential term is very different from the first. A second-term president is freed from many of the political considerations of a first term, because he cannot run for the office again because of the constitutional two-term limit. With some of the political pressure relieved, many presidents spend more time on international affairs than domestic concerns, focusing on building a lasting legacy. It is the last chance for a do-over and, as the years pass in a second term, there is a palpable sense that time is running out to accomplish much of anything. Presidents may feel constrained to behave a certain way or cater to a certain constituency during a first term for political reasons. In a second term, a president is free to show more of his true colors and make compromises or decisions that may be unpopular with his political base. It is the last chance to get it right and get it done.

Reagan followed this playbook. The president became increasingly preoccupied with foreign policy during his second term. One example was his authorization of the bombing of Libya in 1986, in retaliation for a bomb explosion at a Berlin discotheque that injured and killed American servicemen. This foreign policy focus included arms control deals with the Soviet Union. He and Gorbachev met at four summits between 1985 and 1988. The two leaders developed a positive personal relationship and made historic agreements on reducing the number of nuclear weapons. This alliance seemed counterintuitive at the time. Reagan was a well-known anticommunist. Of course, this all took place while Reagan continued the largest peacetime defense buildup in U.S. history, infusing a massive amount of money into defense spending that contributed to the growth of the U.S. budget deficit, even as it imposed tremendous strains on the Soviet Union struggling to keep pace.

With the benefit of hindsight, it is now clear that the Soviets paid a higher price for greater defense spending than did the United States. When Saudi Arabia decided to increase oil production in September 1985, a move designed to increase its market share, the world price of oil dropped because of greater global supply. Oil was a crucial Soviet export. In fact, the Soviet Union was the world's largest producer of oil in 1980. The loss of oil revenue, the high cost of the arms race, and the weight of decades of dysfunction of the centralized communist economic system steadily eroded the strength of the USSR.

Reagan's simultaneous work on arms control and the defense buildup appeared contradictory. East-West tensions grew worse when he moved to put American short-range missiles in Europe, for example. Just at the time Reagan prepared to meet yet again with Gorbachev on nuclear weapons negotiations, the president issued a famous challenge at the Brandenburg Gate on June 12, 1987, near the Berlin Wall, the quintessential symbol of communist oppression and the division between East and West that had endured since the end of World War II. Those engaged in preparing that speech have said that it was intended to encourage Gorbachev to continue down the path of openness and transparency. But it was seen, then and now, as an aggressive challenge to the Soviet leader.

Reagan said, "We welcome change and openness; for we believe that freedom and security go together, that the advance of human liberty can only strengthen the cause of world peace. There is one sign the Soviets can make that would be unmistakable, that would advance dramatically the cause of freedom and peace. General Secretary Gorbachev, if you seek peace, if you seek prosperity for the Soviet Union and Eastern Europe, if you seek liberalization, come here to this gate. Mr. Gorbachev, open this gate. Mr. Gorbachev, tear down this wall." Those words became one of the most famous phrases of his presidency. Ten months after Reagan left office, in November 1989, the Berlin Wall came down.

Reagan's second term was marred by the Iran-Contra affair. Lieutenant Colonel Oliver North, a senior White House national security aide, secretly orchestrated the sale of arms to Iran to generate the cash needed to fund the Contras in Nicaragua, an anticommunist group supported by the CIA. This action violated a specific prohibition imposed by

Congress (the Boland Amendment). The president insisted he knew nothing of the illicit exchange, but Reagan's popularity suffered when an independent investigation confirmed his version of events, showing that he was disengaged from the day-to-day operations of the White House.

In 1980, Reagan had been the oldest president ever elected. While he recovered fully from the assassination attempt in 1981, he experienced other health issues during his tenure. In July 1985, he had a cancerous polyp removed from his large intestine. Mac sent a cactus plant and a Louis L'Amour Western novel to the president at Bethesda Naval Hospital with a note that said, "Someone as tough as you should have something besides posies in the hospital room." Reagan replied just a few days later. "Thanks so much for the tough-looking cactus plant and the Louis L'Amour book—Please know how much I appreciate your continued friendship and concern. Ron." In his own hand, Reagan added a postscript: "I've finished the book already—couldn't put it down."

In 1983, Carol Giacomo, then a *Hartford Courant* correspondent, wrote an article assessing Mac's performance after the first two years of the Reagan administration. She noted, "His leverage within the Administration derives in no small measure from the fact that he has, as many like to say, 'the boss's ear.' When Reagan wants company for a horseback ride, Baldrige is often the one he calls." In fact, Mac and the president did not ride together often, but a photograph circulated of the two of them from behind, headed to the Quantico Marine Corps Base for a ride. It was the contrast between the two that caught the imagination, making it a great photo and perhaps magnifying their relationship. Reagan wore form-fitting jodhpurs, a tight shirt, and formal English riding boots. Next to him, right in step, was Mac, in low-slung, slouchy jeans, cowboy boots, and an old cowboy hat. Despite the misinterpretation of the frequency of their time together on horseback, and their different styles, their relationship was warm. Robert Gray, a legendary Washington lobbyist, told a reporter that Reagan liked Mac right away because, like Reagan, Mac was his own man and straightforward—what you saw was what you got.

This warm relationship remained an advantage for Mac in the ongoing policy battles. By the second term, Mac was also completely comfortable in his role. He had reorganized the Commerce Department to reflect both the priorities of the Reagan administration and his own interest and concern in international trade. While some cabinet secretaries resigned or moved to different positions, Mac stayed right where he was. He liked the job and had managed to use the tools at his disposal to mold trade policy. He was also now experienced in the ways of Washington.

The second term began with sadness, however. His father, Howard Malcolm Baldrige Sr., died at the Lutheran Home in Southbury, Connecticut, at the age of ninety after a long illness. Mac mourned but did not dwell on his personal loss, because the job remained as challenging and demanding as ever with twelve-hour days, six-day weeks, and a busy social schedule.

Protectionist fervor in Congress grew steadily in tandem with a trade deficit that increased exponentially with every passing year, despite Mac's best efforts. There were months and quarters when the trade deficit seemed to be leveling off or even improving, but the improvements proved to be momentary blips. While some of this was because of the value of the dollar, the trend toward a permanent and significant trade imbalance was unmistakable. There were dire implications that the United States might become a permanent debtor nation and customer instead of a provider of goods and services. What could not be fully understood at the time was that the onset of globalization had inextricably changed the world economic dynamic. In the future, a trade deficit would not mean the same as it had in the past. There were too many other factors at work, including the changes under way in the economic structures of the so-called developed world. The United States would never completely lose its industrial base, as was feared, but the core of its economy became more diversified over time. For example, high-technology, intellectual property (particularly American movies and recordings), and services became enormously valuable exports. No one could anticipate in the 1980s that thirty years in the future, the United States would be the only superpower left in the world, yet still burdened with both dramatically high budget and trade deficits. It is now apparent that the economic world order was in flux and the traditional way of analyzing the domestic economy would radically change as the global economy became more linked and interdependent. Mac had a sense of this. In one interview, he expressed confidence that the United States would still be a strong industrial power in twenty years, but he could not say what that would look like. No one could; the world was changing very quickly.

President Reagan recognized the political reality of the time. Congress was not only becoming more protectionist every year but also protectionism was increasingly a bipartisan effort. Even his Republican friends were howling for more aggressive action, which could not be ignored. Republican lawmakers were sometimes on opposite sides of the trade issue; while Robert Dole, the Republican senator from Kansas, expressed deep concern about policies that hurt American farmers and their ability to export wheat and corn, his Republican counterparts from North and South Carolina, Jesse Helms and Strom Thurmond, were demanding more protection for textiles, big industries in their home states. It was not a zero-sum game, with gains and losses equally balanced. Europe and China had no qualms about cutting off or restricting imports in one sector of the U.S. economy if they were prohibited or restricted from exporting goods to the United States in another area. In 1983, Bob Dole complained that farmers lost $500 million in wheat sales to China because of restrictions on textile imports.

In the second term, Reagan was also less popular because of the Iran-Contra scandal. His hard-line rhetoric offered little comfort to those who felt they were losing their jobs to foreign competitors. Mac had effectively developed a blueprint for a middle way on international trade in the first term. During his second term, the president moved more openly toward this middle path, which was a more protectionist posture than the pure free traders would have liked. As Reagan embraced the notions of reciprocity and fairness, the stated policy moved away from the unfettered free trade position. Mac and other administration officials insisted that they were only advocating tariffs or bans as a last resort, in response to grievous provocation from foreigners.

The Reagan administration frequently only acted on trade policy changes when forced by the House or Senate. For example, an announcement of an administration trade initiative would come on the eve of a House debate of a trade bill that the administration opposed, or a deal would finally be cut with a trading partner days after the Senate expressed deep unhappiness with the level of imports. The shift in policy was practical and realistic. The most political Reagan administration officials reasoned that a step toward the protectionist side was better than being forced to go too far by a restrictive new law that might trigger a genuine trade war, causing consumer prices to rise and possibly leading to shortages. What emerged during those years was a compromise position that assuaged the critics, and, in Mac's view, looked out for the United States' best economic interests.

Now, thirty years after these events, the push and pull of politics and economic reality is more apparent. Even Japan, in its prime in the mid-1980s, recognized that it had to change some practices to continue to do business with the rest of the world. For example, in 1985, Japan agreed to stop commercial whaling by 1988. Environmentalists had been up in arms over Japanese whaling because their fishing practices were wiping out an entire species of the world's largest mammal. Japan did not so much recognize the environmental concerns as it responded to flat-out threats. If Japan did not agree, the United States threatened to cut off access to half of its offshore fishing quotas in U.S. northern Pacific waters. Fish is an important source of protein in their diet, so the Japanese acquiesced.

In September 1985 in the East Room of the White House, President Reagan announced a new trade policy. The reporters who covered trade issues noted that the intent of this "new" policy was to head off trade legislation on the Hill. From a substantive viewpoint, this policy held little that was really new and different. The president set up a $300 million fund to support U.S. businesses that were being hurt by foreign unfair trade practices. He signaled a willingness to use existing laws and tools to act more aggressively against practices perceived as unfair in the United States. He asked the U.S. trade representative to initiate investigations into a Korean law that prohibited fair competition for U.S. insurance firms, a Brazilian law restricting the sale of U.S. high-tech products, and Japanese restrictions on the sale of U.S. tobacco products. He also ordered the trade representative to accelerate existing probes into European import restrictions on canned fruit and Japanese prohibitions of leather.

In other words, the White House was affirming actions that the Commerce Department and U.S. Trade Representative's office had already begun.

What was more striking was the similarity between Reagan's language at this point and the speeches and remarks Mac had been making for the previous four years. The president's rhetoric signaled a distinct policy shift toward the "fair trade" policy long advocated by his Commerce Secretary. The president reiterated his support for free trade, but he also spoke of fair trade, leveling the playing field, and playing by the rules. He made explicit the need to take action to protect U.S. businesses from foreign competition.

The president said, "Above all else, free trade is, by definition, fair trade . . . I believe that if trade is not fair for all, then trade is free in name only. I will not stand by and watch American businesses fail because of unfair trading practices abroad. I will not stand by and watch American workers lose their jobs because other nations do not play by the rules."

While Reagan is lionized by conservatives today as an icon of modern conservatism, those who worked with him said he did not view a middle course or compromise as a defeat. Reagan wanted to win the Cold War against communism, and he wanted America to prosper. These were not mutually exclusive goals to him. He also could simultaneously believe in free trade as an ideal but make allowances for U.S. interests, just as Mac did.

Pentagon officials continued to fret about the ability of nations in the Soviet bloc to obtain U.S. technology indirectly through the United States' trading partners, who might resell the equipment or even produce their own versions for export. In May 1985, Mac signed an agreement in New Delhi in which India gave assurances that no communist bloc nations would have access to any sophisticated equipment or software that India bought from the United States. These backdoor avenues to the Soviet Union through third parties were troublesome. A poor or developing country would obtain products from the United States and then promptly sell them to another nation in the Soviet bloc. That October, the Reagan administration kept its side of the deal and approved the sale of a wide range of sophisticated equipment to India. Much of it had direct military applications, such as a radar system and six super minicomputers. Of course, the Reagan administration was not inclined to give India a blank check. U.S. officials turned down a request for an even more advanced supercomputer because of concerns that the computer might be used for nuclear research, rather than for India's stated purpose, weather research.

In September 1986, the trade deficit narrowed to $12.6 billion. It was the best showing in five months, and Mac described it as "turning the corner" in the trade deficit. In fact, the improvement was because of a 300 percent decline in the value of the dollar, which discouraged American purchases overseas and increased foreign orders for American-made products. The value of the dollar was a key factor in the trade balance, but it was only one factor. The developing world was discovering the advantages of manufacturing for their own domestic economies. Big factories created jobs for their own citizens who, just a few years earlier, had barely scratched out livings as subsistence farmers. American and multinational companies quickly discovered they could reduce their overhead and the cost of production by locating a plant in a low-wage developing country rather than in a small town in the United States of America. This trend grew during the final decades of the twentieth century.

The third year of a presidential term is usually the last significant opportunity for a president to pass a major bill or launch a key initiative. In the fourth year, an election year, the legislative process slows down and sometimes comes to a halt. Candidates for reelection tend to get preoccupied with political concerns and are reluctant to vote on controversial items. If a president is nearing the end of eight years in office, the opposition party, hopeful that the White House will change hands in the next election, drags its collective feet to slow legislation to give the new president a fresh start, free of the policies of his predecessor. After years of service in government, cabinet officials and senior staff begin to drift away in pursuit of their postgovernment careers. Some leave early to get a head start. Others burn out. This can be disruptive and create a temporary vacuum of power and experience. The window began to close on Reagan's ability to affect major changes in 1987. Mac, then at the height of his influence and experience as a cabinet secretary, was ready. In March 1987, the Reagan administration took several steps that were the culmination of Mac Baldrige's work in Washington.

Iran wanted to buy computers from Digital Equipment Corporation (DEC) of Maynard, Massachusetts. DEC was one of the first major computer companies in the United States and made its mark selling one of the first popularly available desktop computers. In 1984, the United States had banned the export of any goods to Iran that could be used by the military. The DEC computers were unsophisticated machines that Iran could easily have obtained from other sources in other countries. Mac felt strongly that Iran was going to buy the computers anyway and that they might as well get them from an American company as one in France or Germany. The Defense Department was dead set against the sale.

The Commerce Department was about to approve export licenses for the computers in early March when Defense Secretary Weinberger became so upset that he asked that the National Security Council take up the issue and that President Reagan himself decide if the sale should go forward. Weinberger had been making this argument for years, but this time the Defense Department's argument was undermined by the fact that Reagan's National Security Council staff had secretly arranged for the clandestine sale of weapons to Iran in the Iran-Contra scheme. The DEC computers were intended for use in electric power production and for the Iranian press agency. It was hard to argue against their sale when the U.S. government had clandestinely sold Hawk anti-aircraft missiles and TOW antitank missiles to Iran for use in the Iran-Iraq War.

Mac had been winning these sorts of battles on a case-by-case basis, but by 1987 it was becoming apparent he was winning the policy war. Donald Lambro, a nationally syndicated columnist, wrote, "Commerce Secretary Malcolm Baldrige is winning his battle within the administration to substantially ease restrictive export regulations that have contributed greatly to America's trade deficits." Senior White House sources told Lambro that the top administration officials were "overwhelmingly" on Mac's side in his battle over exports with the Pentagon. Mac argued that excessive export controls hurt the United States' competitiveness. "This is not a zero sum game," said Mac. "The overall security of this country is comprised of both economic and military security." Mac made the case that export controls were more damaging to the defense industrial base. Foreign nations were increasingly opting to use products produced by other countries because of the uncertainty of getting American goods due to national security restrictions. With international markets drying up, American manufacturers were hard-pressed to stay in business if forced to rely exclusively upon the U.S. market. Mac's argument for these sales was growing more sophisticated, more nuanced, and more convincing.

During that same month of March 1987, the ongoing struggle with Japan became more intense. A series of separate Japanese actions created a critical mass that finally tipped the precarious balance established by endless negotiations and discussions over the previous few years. Fujitsu tried to purchase Fairchild Semiconductor Company at the same time that Japanese officials decided to limit to 10 percent the participation of U.S. and British firms in a telecommunications consortium, instead of the 30 percent allowed by Japanese law. The major telecom firms in Great Britain and the United States had been eager to get a foothold in the Japanese market. Earlier that month, Japan also thwarted a bid by Motorola, the Illinois company that created the first handheld portable telephone, to sell its car phones in Japan.

Japan's ongoing reluctance to open up its markets to foreign competition grated on American officials. Mac testified on the Hill that month about the critical importance of Japan opening up its markets, and he made it clear that he and other officials were running out of patience. He went so far as to deem the recent semiconductor agreement negotiated with Japan a failure because of Japanese intransigence. On March 23, the *Financial Times* reported that tensions between the two countries were at the "breaking point" and Japan, increasingly concerned about the heightened rhetoric coming from U.S. officials, formally asked the U.S. government not to impose sanctions.

On March 28, President Reagan lowered the boom. He imposed a 100 percent tariff on $300 million worth of Japanese products including computers, disc drives, color and black-and-white television sets, tape players, floppy discs, power hand tools, and x-ray film. It was the first significant retaliatory move against the Japanese by the United States and was scheduled to take effect in mid-April, just before the Japanese prime minister was supposed to meet with Reagan in Washington. The message was loud, clear, and utterly shocking to the Japanese, who apparently thought they could continue to muddle along giving rhetorical support to the idea of opening their markets while keeping them closed to most foreign goods and services. The tariffs were a direct response to Japan's refusal to honor the trade agreement reached eight months earlier on semiconductor sales.

The reaction to the president's announcement was immediate. The stock market fell as traders feared instability, a drop in profits, and perhaps a trade war. MITI summoned leading Japanese firms to an emergency meeting to ask them to expand purchases of U.S. goods. The United States was invited by the Japanese government to help Japan develop its next generation of fighter planes. Six Japanese semiconductor firms immediately said they would slash their production up to 30 percent and import 10 percent more from the United States.

In many respects, all of the work Mac had been doing since joining the cabinet in 1981 was coming together. As a member of the original Reagan cabinet, he brought experience and relationships to bear, and his practical approach proved its value. "The Secretary had one objective in mind and that was the health of U.S. business—but always tempered with political realities," said Jim Moore.

Mac was not viewed as a navel gazer who brooded over policy or philosophy; yet his peers considered him a visionary. Conservative columnist George Will reportedly once asked Ronald Reagan whom he viewed as true visionaries. He named Jeane Kirkpatrick, the brilliant anticommunist who was the first woman to serve as U.S. ambassador to the United Nations, and Mac Baldrige.

Mac's influence did not go unnoticed. On May 19, 1987, a *New York Times* article noted that he was soon to pass Herbert Hoover as the longest serving Commerce Secretary. Hoover built a national reputation as a reformer when he served as Commerce Secretary under presidents Harding and Coolidge. He used the position as a stepping-stone to the

presidency in 1928. He had the bad luck to be president during the worst economic depression in the nation's history and
lost his second election to Franklin D. Roosevelt in 1932. As
Commerce Secretary, however, historians say that he elevated
the department to the importance of the departments of State
and Treasury. While Mac's Commerce Department never
rivaled State and Treasury in power or importance during the
Reagan years, he did raise the stature of the organization. The
Times article said that the "consensus" of the Reagan cabinet
had moved toward Mac on a "hawkish trade policy." He was
described as the "driving force" on imposition of sanctions
against the Japanese and was credited by many for convincing
Fujitsu to drop its bid to acquire Fairchild by making forceful public statements in opposition. The *Hartford Courant*
reported: "Baldrige has taken a cabinet slot sometimes viewed
as a political throwaway and parlayed it into a position of
respectable clout."

Mac took the long view and did not always win right
away. For example, he began pushing for limits on imports
of machine tools to protect the domestic industry more than
two years before the president ordered the restraints. The
machine tool business is one of those underappreciated
industries that is an economic mainstay in any industrialized
nation. Mac had a particularly keen understanding of the
importance of machine tools (as well as Japan's many nontariff barriers) from his own business background. While the
president initially resisted protectionist measures, Mac's side
eventually prevailed.

Charles Ludolph, a deputy assistant secretary of commerce, was a career civil servant who held a political position under Mac. He said that the change in U.S. trade policy
from the free trade multilateral agreements to a fair trade
policy based upon the principle of reciprocity was a major
achievement for Mac. "This was a huge change in trade pol-

icy," he said. "It required a complete new political consensus in the U.S. making a distinction between protectionism and trade action justified by taking action against free riders and bad actors . . . Baldrige and Brock were a shock to trade policy. Fair trade was new. They were much more aligned with Congress and the politics coming from industry and labor. The challenge was picking the sectors that fair trade can and should help, versus the issues that simply wallowed in protectionism."

In 1987, Mac was at the top of his game and at the zenith of his influence in the government. All was not perfect, however. Early in the year, he was hospitalized for weeks with pneumonia. A lifelong smoker who always kept scrupulously to the president's timetable of one hour for a cabinet meeting so he could go outside to smoke, the pneumonia laid him flat. He grew a beard and mustache during his sickness and returned to work thinner and sporting that mustache, his first facial hair since serving in the military during World War II. He plunged right back into his job.

7

TEXTILES, CHINA, AND THE DEVELOPING WORLD

WHILE MAJOR TRADE ISSUES WITH EUROPE AND JAPAN dominated Mac's time in Washington, he had a keen appreciation of the economic potential of large developing nations like China and India. At that time, their economies were evolving from agriculture to industry. Today both China and India are international economic powerhouses, but in the 1980s, these large Asian nations were known more for population growth and poverty than for economic performance.

China is a case in point. The population of China passed the one billion mark in 1982 to become the most populous nation on earth. The country had recently emerged from the Cultural Revolution imposed by Mao Zedong between 1966 and 1976 to revive the ideological purity of the communist revolution. The Cultural Revolution was a brutal step back in time. It was aggressively anti-intellectual and antimodernity. Industrial production plummeted, and more than 1.5

million people died, including some of the best educated and most highly trained people in the country. China was set back decades economically. Any modernization or economic progress stopped during that decade. The nation could barely feed all of its people (resulting in the adoption of the one-child policy in 1979). It certainly could not compete with other nations in trade. In 1981, a pedestrian on the main street of Beijing would see few automobiles or colored clothing. The teeming throngs wore the same drab brown garments, and streets were packed with thousands of bicycles moving in what seemed to be an uncoordinated rhythm. Communist leaders realized that they had a lot of ground to cover to catch up with the rest of the industrial world, and they were eager to obtain technology and industrial help from the West.

While President Richard M. Nixon had reestablished diplomatic relations with China a decade earlier, China tended to have stronger trade relations with Germany and Russia, where many Chinese officials who were in power at the time had been educated and trained. Mac wanted to change that bias and get American companies into the mix. He, like other Americans, recognized the opportunity inherent in one billion potential customers.

Mac headed to China in May 1982 for the first meeting of the U.S.-China Joint Commission on Commerce and Trade (JCCT), which was to be the main forum for dealing with bilateral issues between the countries. Mac traveled to China twice for annual meetings and twice hosted the Chinese in Washington. The first meeting was the first high-level trade contact between the Americans and the Chinese since a recent flap over the United States providing political asylum to a Chinese defector. The asylum concern was not unusual. There were always complicating issues with China. China was a communist nation and, like the Soviet Union, had domestic policies antithetical to the United States. Like any sovereign nation, China did not welcome another country's interference in its internal politics or with its citizens. The United States had been allowing arms sales to Taiwan, the sovereign state set up in 1949 by the anticommunist government, the Republic of China, after it lost the Chinese civil war to the communists in Mainland China. The issue of official recognition of Taiwan was still a touchy one. The anticommunists in the U.S. government championed the cause of the Republic of China (ROC or Taiwan). The Reagans still entertained Madame Chiang Kai-Shek, known as "the Dragon Lady," the influential American-educated widow of the ROC leader. The United Nations still recognized the ROC and would not seat the People's Republic of China, the mainland communist government (or "Red China" as it was known), until 1991. And the import of Chinese textiles was sharply limited by long-standing quotas imposed by the United States.

Mac wanted the potentially huge Chinese market to be open to American products. He sensed interest from the new generation of Chinese leaders who were taking charge of the government. Many of these new leaders had been educated abroad and recognized the economic price of the Cultural Revolution, and they wanted to move their country forward. The diplomats at the State Department also wanted improved relations with China. In the 1980s, the communists in China were seen as a kind of counterbalance to the communists in the Soviet Union. In the eyes of U.S. diplomats, it made sense to keep these two large nations from forging alliances and combining into a collaborative communist power. Before Mac flew to China for the U.S.-China Joint Commission on Commerce and Trade in May 1984, President Reagan traveled to China and signed agreements allowing U.S. industry to compete for billions of dollars in sales of nuclear technology to China. This nuclear technology was intended to generate electrical power, an essential building block of industrialization.

The trips were grueling but enormously interesting. Few Americans had the opportunity to travel to China, so the trips included many social events and visits to famous Chinese spots, such as the Forbidden City and Tiananmen Square. Midge accompanied Mac on this trip and visited many of the tourist sites while he attended formal meetings. At the Great Wall, Midge and Helen Robbins drew notice from the Chinese because each was a tall woman, towering over the Chinese, and Midge had red hair, something rarely seen in China. Dozens of people trailed them on their tour as if they, too, were a rare sight to behold.

Prior to the trip, the Chinese ambassador in Washington had hosted Mac's delegation for dinner at his embassy. The event was a primer on what to expect on their visit, including a lesson on the cuisine and the preferred liquor of the time in China. The Chinese liked *Moutai,* a potent drink distilled from fermented sorghum that was more than 50 percent alcohol and served in liqueur glasses to be downed in shots. The traditional Chinese, the delegation was told, would stand and tip their glass down at someone at their table, and the etiquette was to join that person in drinking the shot in one gulp. The old Chinese at the dinner, wanting to demonstrate their superiority, tried more than once to trick an American into drinking far too much.

Mac's counterpart, the Chinese Minister for Commerce, made the rounds of the tables with Mac to greet her guests. At one table, she spotted Howard Dixon, who was Mac's personal aide. Howard was a very sophisticated man who once performed the same job for Nelson Rockefeller when he was governor of New York and vice president of the United States. Howard was well traveled and resembled a shorter version of the comedian Bill Cosby, with the same wry grin.

Black people, like redheads, were rarely seen in China, and Howard was the only African American in a room of hundreds at this dinner.

The minister tipped her glass at Howard, an invitation to drink, but Howard did not drink alcohol, so he politely and smilingly refused. There was a standoff of several minutes before the minister continued on her table rounds, while Mac watched the exchange with some amusement.

Mac set in motion a major program to support U.S. exports to China and to make it easier for U.S. goods and services to be used to improve the economic infrastructure of the country. China seemed to need everything to build up its industrial capacity—roads, energy plants, manufacturing plants, and mining facilities—and it wanted it all yesterday. Christian R. Holmes, the director of the U.S. Trade and Development Agency, put the plan into operation. The Commerce Department had commercial service experts based in Beijing, a staff that had been shifted from the State Department to Commerce as part of the Carter administration reorganization. These experts identified large-scale construction projects on the Chinese wish list that might hold potential for U.S. goods and services. The U.S. Trade and Development Agency awarded a grant to the Chinese to conduct a feasibility study with one major condition: the work had to be performed by a U.S. firm. "We would sit down with the Chinese and say, 'We understand you want to build a dam. We will get you a grant to plan construction of the dam on the condition you award it to a U.S. firm. We want the specifications written to U.S. standards so when you buy equipment, you will buy it in America,'" explained Holmes. The American companies not only listed U.S. specifications and U.S. products in their feasibility studies but developed positive working relationships with those Chinese officials who would eventually make the critical procurement decisions to get the projects built. This scheme worked beautifully. The Commerce Department funded about one hundred different projects in China that generated almost $1 billion in the export of U.S. goods and services associated with the planning, design, construction, and operation of the projects, including major energy, transportation, and metallurgy projects. Hard-liners were dismayed by U.S. sales to "Red China," and columnists like Jack Anderson, the syndicated investigative journalist, all but named Mac and others involved in improving trade with China as traitors. Most businessmen, however, were delighted, because the Chinese work represented American jobs and profits.

The Commerce Department frequently hosted delegations of Chinese leaders in Washington. Jim Moore remembers holding an early luncheon for a delegation of Chinese leaders, all dressed in drab Mao suits, at the elegant Hay-Adams Hotel near the White House. "The Chinese did not appreciate or understand Western culture," said Moore. "The old Chinese way of showing appreciation was to pass gas. I will never forget the expressions on the faces of the waiters as they went in and out of this small private dining room" while the grateful Chinese showed their appreciation for the lovely meal.

"Mac brought tolerance to the table," with the Chinese, said Holmes. "He would smile shyly and be understanding. He was a balanced, moderate and tolerant man with a good commercial instinct. A lot of other people would not have been able to handle it in that way."

The U.S. Trade and Development Agency operated the same program in other Southeastern Asian nations, particularly in Thailand, where the program opened up major inroads for American firms in the coal and electric power sectors. Mac worked hard to ease restrictions on imports of South Korean products, including steel and color television sets, in 1981.

The color TVs attracted the most negative attention in news accounts, but Mac recognized the value of making trade more profitable for the South Koreans from both diplomatic and economic standpoints. The United States had been supporting South Korea militarily since the Eisenhower administration, and theirs was an important strategic friendship.

For all the rhetoric about "free trade" from Reagan administration officials, there was a glaring exception and politically untouchable example of protectionism that existed before, during, and after the administration: quotas on imports of textiles. Mac was not someone given to fretting over inconsistencies in policy, and there is no indication that the blatant protectionism of the textile quota system gave him any great concern. Ever pragmatic, he accepted it as something he could not change in the short run. But he did play a key role in getting rid of the system in the long run by helping to launch the international trade talks that came to be called the Uruguay Round.

The American textile industry dates back to the earliest years of the Republic. The first automated yarn-spinning mill was built in Pawtucket, Rhode Island, in 1792. Francis Cabot Lowell, a wealthy early industrialist from Newburyport, Massachusetts, built the first integrated textile mill on the Charles River in Waltham, Massachusetts, not far from Boston. After the War of 1812, Lowell was among those pushing to convince Congress to impose protectionist taxes on British-finished cloth as part of the Tariff of 1816, the first tariff passed by Congress to explicitly protect fledgling U.S. industries from foreign competition. The British had flooded the United States with reduced-price goods, intending to drive their U.S. competitors out of business. The tariff imposed a 25 percent duty on cotton and woolen imports for three years. Lowell died a year later at the age of forty-two; his business associates built an entire mill town north of

Boston on the Merrimack River and called it Lowell in his honor. The city of Lowell became known as the cradle of the Industrial Revolution in America, as the first large-scale factory town in the country. It was also the birthplace of the American labor movement. The mill girls, young Yankee farm women who worked in the mills, mounted an early labor protest when the mill owners tried to cut their pay by 15 percent during the economic depression in the 1830s.

Textiles enjoyed a national constituency from the start, because the cotton that was taken to the mills in the North to be turned into finished fabric was grown in the South. During the first and second world wars in the twentieth century, naval blockades limited imports from Europe and fueled a drive for self-sufficiency, strikingly similar to conditions during the War of 1812 a hundred years earlier. After World War II, the invention and proliferation of fabrics like rayon, nylon, and polyester gave new life to the apparel and fabric industries.

While the United States strongly supported free trade as an ideal after World War II, the textile lobby made sure that textiles maintained official protection. In the 1950s, the administration of Dwight D. Eisenhower negotiated a "voluntary agreement" limiting imports of cotton textile products from Hong Kong, India, Japan, and Pakistan. By 1961, the John F. Kennedy administration had negotiated short-term protective quotas as part of an update of the General Agreement on Tariffs and Trade (GATT), the trade agreements first negotiated in 1947 to guarantee free trade throughout the world after World War II. In 1962, the Kennedy administration replaced the short-term agreement with a long-term arrangement that expanded the quotas. In 1974, those quotas were expanded beyond cotton to include synthetic fabrics.

President Reagan, like the presidents who came before him, bowed to the political realities of the textile lobby. The textile industry was treated as special by the government. There were government officials who did nothing but focus on textile imports. The U.S. Trade Representative's office included an ambassador for textiles until the late 1990s. The Commerce Department had a deputy assistant secretary who worked only on textiles. The quota system was the elephant in the room: the protectionist policy was at odds with the free trade goals and rhetoric of the Reagan administration, but this dissonance was rarely the subject of any debate. Roger Milliken, an heir to a textile fortune and a prominent businessman, was a major Republican contributor and could get the ears of high-ranking officials in the Reagan administration, according to Lionel Olmer. Powerful lawmakers, such as senators Edward M. Kennedy of Massachusetts and Ernest "Fritz" Hollings of South Carolina, were diligent in looking out for the textile workers and manufacturers in their states. About 850,000 Americans worked in the industry at the time. Hollings invariably launched into a lengthy diatribe about the horrors of importing textiles at the start of congressional hearings on trade, according to Tom Collamore. Olmer says that the Reagan administration was determined to avoid problems with Congress whenever possible and had to pick its battles. Collamore bluntly says, "On textiles, domestic politics trumped the larger 'free' trade drumbeat."

Mac did not spend a lot of time dealing with textile quotas. As a pragmatist, he appreciated that he would get little accomplished on Capitol Hill if he picked a fight he could not win. Because of the geographic distribution of the textile and apparel industries in the United States, the support for quotas was bipartisan and widespread. The Reagan administration negotiated a six-year agreement with Hong Kong in 1982 that limited the growth of imports in sensitive categories. The administration was attempting to negotiate the same terms with Korea and Taiwan, and news reports speculated that similar deals would be struck with India, Thailand, the Philippines, and China.

Paul O'Day, now the longtime president and counsel for the American Fiber Manufacturers Association, was the top textile expert in the government when Reagan took office, and he worked closely with Mac. O'Day served in the government for more than twenty-five years in a number of high-ranking positions, including deputy assistant secretary for trade development and textiles. Without the quotas, he was convinced that the U.S. industry "would have collapsed like a poked balloon."

O'Day wielded extraordinary power under the terms of an executive order issued by Richard Nixon many years before. The executive order created an interagency committee, chaired by the Department of Commerce, which administered textile and apparel quotas. As chairman, at any time he could unilaterally prevent or allow imports of more than one hundred categories of textiles, with a majority vote of the committee, which was stacked in favor of U.S. business and labor interests. "We could do pretty much anything we wanted, and we would watch imports very carefully and act week to week," he said.

But O'Day was instinctively cautious. His career in government had begun in 1959 as a patent examiner in the Eisenhower administration. He had no desire to rock the boat or use his authority any more than necessary, and he was fully aware of the "free trade" mantra of the Reagan administration ideologues. He asked Mac to judge his performance "'by how seldom you see me. When you see me, there will be a problem.' I worked hard so that things would never get to a level where he would have to be involved." From all indications, Mac liked that arrangement and agreed with the even-handed approach. O'Day kept textile imports steady; the level of imports was the same on the day he left the position as on the day he began. This was by design. Sticking with the status quo kept all the various constituencies somewhat peaceful. Keeping the issue under the news radar allowed the Secretary to focus his time and attention on the more pressing trade issues of the day. At that time, America's competitiveness in electronics, high-technology, and the emerging computer field was far more important to the future of the nation than textiles and apparel production. Textile issues rarely made headlines during Mac's time in office.

While the Reagan administration accepted textile quotas as a domestic political necessity, the administration resisted when the industry tried to flex its muscle and pushed for even more protection, exceeding the tolerance of President Reagan. In December 1987, five months after Mac's death, the president vetoed a massive global trade bill that would have placed even stricter limits on textiles from a dozen countries, mostly in Asia. Although proponents of the stricter quotas waited until August 1988, an election year, to try to override the veto, it fell eight votes short of an override in the U.S. House.

Textile quotas caused some unexpected developments in those years when American industry was just beginning to move jobs overseas to take advantage of lower production costs. While it was not the intent of this policy to help poor countries develop an industrial base, the quotas had this unexpected benefit for some of the poorest countries. When limits on trade were imposed on the more efficient producers, manufacturers sought other locations, without such limits, in which to build their plants. As a result, the textile industry grew in Vietnam, Pakistan, Bangladesh, El Salvador, the Dominican Republic, and Honduras, which were desperately poor nations at that time, with few opportunities for employment and production.

Eventually, in 2005, the tariff quotas that had been in force for 188 years went away. Those seeds were planted during the Reagan administration by Mac, U.S. Trade Representative Clayton Yeutter (who replaced Bill Brock in 1985), and Agriculture Secretary Dick Lyng (who replaced Jack Block in 1986), with the launch of the Uruguay Round of GATT (the General Agreement on Tariffs and Trade) talks in Punta del Este in 1986.

The pace of globalization in the 1980s took place so quickly that the round of GATT talks completed at the end of the Carter administration could not adequately deal with all of the issues arising over trade. The United States had some keen concerns. The old agreements dealt primarily with commodities, but services, intellectual property, and high-technology were becoming just as crucial to the U.S. economy. The United States produced intellectual property (more than music and Hollywood movies) that eventually would be very important to the economy. The computer, software, and high-tech industry may have been in its infancy, but it was clear to Mac that this was the industry of the future for the United States. Increasingly, nontariff barriers obstructed the sale of these items overseas. One article from 1983 noted that it was illegal to broadcast a television commercial in Australia that had been made outside its borders. This rule forced U.S. companies to make their commercials for Australia in that country, giving jobs and services to Australian actors and film-related workers. In Canada, banks headquartered in other countries were required to maintain and process all data within Canadian borders. These were not irrational rules, but they were restrictions on the U.S. industries that were growing, and GATT did not address them at all.

The Uruguay Round of GATT launched in the resort town of Punta del Este, which was a rocking, lively town in tourist season, with gorgeous beaches and plentiful casinos. The Round launched in the off-season, so there was sufficient hotel space for all participants. It was a dark, quiet, deserted place in those days, with little to do except focus on the job at hand—the trade talks—and, in the limited free time, shop for the bulky hand-knit sweaters for which the region was famous.

The strains between the haves and the have-nots, the developed and developing countries, were apparent from the start. The United States and Europe already had the infrastructure and means to dominate international commerce. That is not to say that the United States and Europe did not have disagreements. Both sides were eager to protect their own industries, including agricultural production, as much as possible. But the developing countries, the Group of 77, were just getting started and did not want to be blocked from developing their own manufacturing economies by these trade agreements.

Mac spent a lot of time in Uruguay trying to calm the concerns of officials from physically large but financially lagging nations, such as India and Brazil, who worried about being steamrolled by the dominant developed nations. They worried that multinational service firms in areas like banking, shipping, and insurance would overwhelm their own domestic companies. Brazil, India, and ten allied countries did not even want services included in the talks, but Mac pushed for inclusion. Former Under Secretary for International Trade Bruce Smart remembers that Mac took it upon himself to reassure officials in the developing countries about the benefit of the trade agreement over the long run. If they opened their markets to American high-technology, they would have greater opportunities to sell textiles and shoes in the United States. This argument had a lot of merit for the United States. Despite the dislocation of losing some manufacturing concerns, particularly in textiles and shoes that were already moving overseas, the United States would benefit in the long run by specializing in the more sophisticated products needed by the developing world. If those developing countries could become more stable by setting up plants that made shoes or underwear, the United States and the rest of the world would benefit from that political and economic stability. History has repeatedly demonstrated that desperate poverty and lack of opportunity fuel terrorism and extremism. It has been true in recent years with Islamic extremists, and it was true in the twentieth century with socialists and communists.

Whether he was in Washington or in Punta del Este, Mac instinctively recognized the merit of extending the courtesy of a personal visit and making an effort to show respect to those who needed to be reassured or persuaded. "He said we are going to make a trip. We are going to go over and call on the Brazilians and the Indians and talk to them about this trade agreement. We will go to their offices," said Smart. "As a result of that extension of cordiality and friendship they dropped their objections to the Uruguay Round and it was a success."

The Uruguay Round was the eighth round of GATT talks post–World War II, when international organizations and accords were negotiated in the hope of fostering enough understanding and communication to avoid a third world war. The Uruguay Round of talks became the largest and most sweeping talks ever undertaken, involving 123 countries, including many small and poor nations. Agreements were based on reciprocity and even-handed treatment between member nations. If the United States gave the European Union a deal on services, it needed to do the same for countries in Africa or Asia. Disagreements needed to be worked out in negotiation aimed at achieving consensus. Transparency was required.

The negotiations in Punta del Este were difficult ones, and the talks did not end there. Mac acknowledged at the time that the battles would not be quickly resolved. Self-interest was a powerful force, and it was no easy thing to strike the balance between all of the competing costs and benefits. He told reporters that the United States still had "a long, long way to go" before the issues would be resolved. The trade ministers assumed it would take four years of talks to reach consensus. It took almost twice as long.

The tradeoffs envisioned by Mac at the start of the talks in 1986 were apparent in the final deal in 1994. Textile quotas were on their way to becoming history in the United States. Intellectual property finally had the same status as corn or steel. The final deal was struck in April 1994, almost seven years after Mac's death. The agreement signed in Marrakesh, Morocco, created the World Trade Organization (WTO), an international institution dealing with trade, investment, and commodity agreements, as well as business practices and government policies that limited trade. A WTO-type organization had been envisioned in the 1940s, but the U.S. Congress refused to approve it at that time. The creation of the World Trade Organization established an international institution to govern trade throughout the world and to officially crack down on dumping, discourage excessive subsidies, and open the doors for all types of products and services to be bought and sold throughout the world.

It is impossible to say if Mac envisioned that outcome as he labored for U.S. interests in Punta del Este in 1986, but it can be said that the outcome reflected his style, his priorities, and his belief that robust trade was good for America and its friends around the world.

8

MANAGEMENT
AND OPERATIONS
AT COMMERCE

THE RESPONSIBILITIES OF THE COMMERCE SECRETARY extended far beyond Mac's interest in international trade because of the plethora of agencies in his domain. Dealing with patents, trademarks, fish quotas, and the radio and television spectrum was not glamorous and rarely made newspaper headlines, but it was an essential part of his charge of looking out for the best interests of American business. As the primary business advocate in Reagan's cabinet, Mac set about making the entire Department more efficient, more effective, and more attuned to business and its needs. This involved imprinting his management style on the entire Department, as well as dealing with some big problems in some of the less exciting agencies within Commerce.

Mac realized that reducing costs and improving services to business were essential to his aims. Modernization and cooperation were two goals that he set for the Commerce

Department. In the 1980s, the government lagged behind the private sector in both areas. Despite the fundamental difference between government (serving the public) and businesses (making profits), Mac believed that good management was the same across sectors. The challenge was considerable. Unlike some other cabinet departments, such as Defense or State, Commerce lacked a single unified purpose. *Government Executive* magazine was brutal and blunt in describing the Commerce Department. "In 1980, the Department of Commerce was simply a feudal kingdom with a large number of separate and independent duchies. Historically lacking definition, the Department grew over the decades mostly as a dumping ground for an odd assortment of government functions. If it were run at all, it was as a loose and shaky holding company. The Department was top heavy in structure and overhead, its fragmented management information systems did not serve central management and no means of systematic planning and follow-up existed." Unbowed by the challenge, Mac believed he could draw upon his experience as a business executive and inspire the career Commerce Department employees to change and improve.

Arlene Triplett, Mac's first Assistant Secretary for Administration, said her boss approached the Commerce Department job in 1981 the same way a new CEO would approach the task of turning around a major private company. He got rid of the departments and functions that did not contribute to the core of the Commerce Department's mission to advocate for business. He set up a management system that built accountability into the bureaucracy. There were specific performance measures linked to reviews and promotions. In her view, this system only worked because Mac himself was committed to it. Other Departments tried to do the same but failed, because their leaders were neither personally engaged nor invested in making the management system work. "Mac was sensitive to this idea that Commerce was a second-class agency," she said. "While he never did anything transparent in terms of increasing the prestige of the Commerce Department, he effectively did it by making the people who worked there feel good about themselves because they worked in a Department led by a very competent and exciting leader." She described his management style this way: "He delegated, but he kept you on a chain. He did not just turn it over. But he did not second guess. He was great to work for. The one time he disagreed with something I suggested, I walked out of the room and realized he was right."

Triplett acted as Mac's point person to improve the operation of the Department. A new management system was put together piecemeal. For financial reasons, it was not possible to introduce a complete new system, so she and her team identified the most effective systems, drew upon existing data in a new way, and constructed a system that built accountability into the bureaucracy.

In Washington, this was considered astonishing. Mac's goals when he took office in 1981 were to develop the best internal management systems in the federal government by 1985 and to substantially upgrade the Department's technical and organizational capabilities to improve services at reduced cost. He dispatched selected career Commerce employees to IBM, Xerox, Hewlett-Packard, 3M, Intel, and Emerson Electric, then considered the best-managed corporations, to discover for themselves how the private sector treated similar management problems. His faith in career government employees and their ability to perform at high levels was rewarded by hard work and superior performance.

Mac established a Department-wide management planning system with twenty major long-term goals, all meant to improve services and advocacy for business. Each agency developed its own specific goals that fed into those priority tasks.

Each goal had specific annual milestones. Managers would pay a price for not meeting these goals. Their promotions and pay were tied to performance. The entire system was linked to the budget process. It was impossible (for budgetary and practical reasons) to reinvent the wheel and introduce an entirely new system to the Department, so his team analyzed elements of existing management systems and used those that either produced the best data or were most effective.

Twenty-eight Commerce Department centers scattered around the country processed administrative payments for everything from purchase orders of envelopes to travel. The new Secretary consolidated all of these into a single management service center in suburban Maryland. Triplett said, "Commerce had eight payroll systems when we got there. We consolidated them all into one at NOAA. Then we asked the Department of Agriculture to run our payroll." When Commerce used the Agriculture Department's National Finance System, personnel costs per payment dropped from $29 to $6. Travel vouchers were paid within three days instead of three weeks. "There was no reason why a Department with a better system could not do it. It was an integration of government functions. OMB ordered others to follow that example," said Triplett. Better management of the Department translated into better service for business and the public. The Office of Management and Budget was so impressed that the agency chief hired Triplett to introduce the same practices throughout the rest of government.

Mac also oversaw the automation of the export licensing system as part of his challenge that the divisions of Commerce operate more like business and be more responsive to business needs. Even as he went out of his way to forge alliances with other cabinet secretaries on issues, he used his influence to force more cooperation between the bureaucrats who could be more vicious in their rivalries than the politicians.

He found the rivalries between government entities thankless, often pointless, and always wasteful. He got involved when NOAA and the Federal Aviation Administration began to battle over weather radar systems, and he forced them to cooperate. Olin Wethington, the Deputy Under Secretary for Trade, said that business interests became elevated as a core foreign policy interest during Mac's tenure. Some of that related to the transfer of the State Department's commercial interest personnel to the Commerce Department at the end of the Carter administration. But Mac made certain that the well-being of U.S. businesses was considered on a par with conventional diplomatic issues in debates over policy. His senior staff quickly realized that Mac was an activist and that he would carry issues to the very top in cabinet meetings, so Wethington hired a team of policy staffers to work on hot-button issues to keep the Secretary prepared with the best arguments and the latest data.

The Patent and Trademark Office (PTO) provides a case study in how Mac used the tools available to the Commerce Department to improve conditions for U.S. business. When Mac took office, the PTO was a mess, plagued by long, unacceptable delays in approving patents and trademarks and stymied by outdated practices, a staff shortage, an inadequate budget, and the total absence of modern technology. Gerry McKiernan often accompanied Mac on many lobbying trips to Capitol Hill. He said that while Mac's primary priority was trade, "he got it done" on the patent side, too. Mac understood the importance of patents through his experience at Scovill. Yale Locks, a Scovill subsidiary and one of the oldest lock companies in the United States, would not have existed without patent protection of the pin tumbler lock and other innovations.

The Patent and Trademark Office can trace its origins directly to the U.S. Constitution. The first citizens of the

United States were farmers and small businessmen. They were as highly motivated by financial concerns, including the high level of taxation levied by the king of England, as they were by a yearning for independence and freedom. Even in those earliest years of the republic, there was a keen appreciation for inventors and their clever innovations.

Benjamin Franklin, one of the most prolific and enterprising men of his era, invented many practical household items, ranging from bifocals and the lightning rod to the Franklin stove. While he never sought a patent for a single invention in the public-spirited interest of making his innovations available to everyone, his fellow Founding Fathers recognized the importance of protecting the rights of inventors. Article 1, Section 8, Clause 8 of the Constitution charges the Congress with promoting "the progress of science and useful arts by securing for limited times to inventors the exclusive right to their respective discoveries." This is a crucial responsibility, because it protects the creation of new products as well as new uses for old ones. Innovation and creativity are the bedrock of American ingenuity and economic success, and giving inventors and entrepreneurs a guarantee of exclusivity for their products for a fixed period of time gives them and future generations an incentive to continue to push the frontiers of discovery. Patents and trademarks provide a level of financial stability and a shot at what can be significant profits. In a capitalist system, those profits can be reinvested into the economy, generating more jobs, more profit, and more inventions.

When Ronald Reagan took office, the Patent and Trademark Office faced years of application backlogs; it was drowning in paperwork. In a speech to the American Bar Association in August 1981, Gerald J. Mossinghoff, the Commissioner of Patents and Trademarks, said more than two hundred thousand patent applications and one hundred thousand trademark applications were then pending and in need of review. The system, created prior to World War II, used techniques based solely on paper searches to determine legitimacy for patents and trademarks. For every single application, a patent investigator had to plow through rooms full of file cabinets and boxes. This meant it took about three years to get a patent registered and more than two years to register a trademark. The system was entirely on paper, and approximately 7 percent of the patents were missing from examiners' files. Because of a shortage of typists, formal opinions were still written in longhand. The workload was daunting. As described by Mossinghoff, the PTO mailroom handled twenty thousand pieces of mail per day, the same number handled by a large suburban post office. If the 108,000 patent applications received each year were stacked up, the stack would be taller than the combined heights of the Empire State Building and the Washington Monument. The quantity and size of those files was expected to double by the turn of the century. In June 1980, the presidential election year, just before the U.S. Supreme Court took its summer break, the Court expanded the scope of items that could be patented to include genetically modified organisms. A genetic engineer who worked for General Electric had tried to patent a bacterium he invented that was capable of breaking down crude oil. The bacterium, a tremendous innovation in fighting oil spills, was intended to gobble up the crude oil spilled in waterways. A patent examiner rejected the application, because at the time, living things, which included bacteria, could not be patented. The court ruling opened the way for patents to be granted in the then-fledgling biotechnology industry, in computer software, genetic technology, and even in business and financial methods.

The pace of inventions was accelerating at that time because of technology. CNN (Cable News Network) was then the only news network on cable and was still in its infancy, but there were indications that all forms of communication would become faster in the future. Technological breakthroughs could be outpaced by innovations in a short period of time, so the need for timely approval of trademarks and inventions was more pressing. There was a compelling need for major change; an NBC magazine show that aired in December 1980 described the patent system as "a cruel hoax."

Patent lawyers and other specialists in the field knew the system was broken, and in 1981 they came up with an idea of how to capture the attention of the new Commerce Secretary. Mossinghoff, then a government lawyer whose service dated back to the Eisenhower administration, had spent twenty years working at the National Aeronautics and Space Administration (NASA) where he had become close friends with Harrison "Jack" Schmitt, the first scientist to fly in space. Schmitt resigned from NASA to run for public office and won election to the U.S. Senate from New Mexico in 1976. Senator Schmitt served on the Senate Committee that held Mac's confirmation hearing as Commerce Secretary. As a member of Schmitt's "kitchen cabinet" of informal advisers, Mossinghoff prepared a list of serious problems (the so-called dirty dozen) at the PTO for the senator to use in questioning the nominee. One item noted that three large conference rooms at the Crystal City, Virginia, patent headquarters, all carefully identified by room number, were filled from floor to ceiling and wall to wall with unopened mail patent applications. Another item said that the patent examiners wrote by hand their recommendations on applications, because there were no typists. Schmitt asked Mac if he was aware of these problems. Mac was shocked. As a businessman, the idea of not responding to customers' mail or not being able to have a document typed was hard to comprehend. Mac went privately to the senator after the hearing to ask him if things were as bad as those anecdotes indicated and to get more information. Schmitt recommended that he talk to Mossinghoff. He did, and Mac eventually asked Mossinghoff, one of the many career employees he elevated to a top job, to serve as Commissioner of Patents and Trademarks during the first Reagan term.

Mossinghoff agreed to take the job on the condition that he would report directly to Mac instead of going through an Assistant Secretary, the reporting line in effect at that time. Mossinghoff had been in government long enough to know that he needed direct access to the top man if he were to remake the long-neglected Patent and Trademark Office. Mac readily agreed to the condition. Change is never easy, and the revolutionary change needed at the PTO promised to be challenging and difficult for the employees. Mac never stood on ceremony, and he preferred to deal directly with key staff. This direct pipeline proved to be invaluable. Mossinghoff was able to speak directly to the Secretary about obstacles and problems, and Mac, informed of problems in a timely way, got personally involved in fixing them.

The Commerce Department needed authorization from Congress for an overhaul of the PTO. The linchpin on the Hill was Representative Jack Brooks, a crusty, cigar-smoking veteran Democratic lawmaker from Texas, who was vehemently anti-Reagan. But nothing could be done without his support. Mac invited the congressman to breakfast. They ate bacon, eggs, and home fries at the Commerce Department from 7:30 until 9:15 a.m., talking all the while, according to Gerry McKiernan, Commerce's legislative liaison. By the time breakfast ended and McKiernan drove Brooks back to his office on the Hill, the deal was done and Brooks was on board.

President Reagan had an interest in the subject of intellectual property. Mossinghoff remembers a courtesy meeting with Mac and President Reagan in the Oval Office in 1981, just before Mossinghoff's nomination as Commissioner of Patents and Trademarks. Mossinghoff later wrote that he was impressed by how much President Reagan knew about the importance of intellectual property. Reagan told the story about Charles Holland Duell, a patent commissioner at the turn of the nineteenth century, who allegedly urged President McKinley to shut down the Patent Office because "everything that can be invented has been invented." In an essay Mossinghoff wrote many years later for the Reagan Presidential Library, he stated, "President Reagan, tongue in cheek, told me not to follow that example and not to make such a recommendation to him while he was President."

According to Mossinghoff, Mac told him that President Reagan viewed intellectual property protection as the key to American competitiveness. The president had a particular interest in copyrights because of his experience as a movie actor. American movies and music were then, as now, among the most counterfeited American products in the world, and this piracy cost the industry enormous amounts of money.

With President Reagan determined to reduce domestic spending and OMB director David Stockman slashing domestic budgets, the likelihood was slim that the administration would ask Congress to appropriate the money needed to automate the Patent Office systems and to recruit and hire the highly trained staff needed to reduce the backlog. The annual budget for the Patent Office was only $79 million at the time. The Defense Department was spared from budget cuts in an administration determined to win the Cold War against the Soviet Union, so all the domestic agencies took a bigger hit. At the time, however, the application filing fee for a patent or trademark was nominal, only $65, just enough to discourage eccentric cranks from filing dozens of meaningless applications but not nearly enough to cover the cost of a professional review of a worthwhile application. Moreover, all of that revenue went directly to the U.S. Treasury into the general fund. Mossinghoff suggested increasing the fee, making it a "user fee," and using that revenue to finance the Patent Office. Historically, anti-tax politicians have gotten around the shortage-of-revenue problem by raising and levying "fees" on various government services. In return for the user fee, Mossinghoff proposed setting a goal of reducing application review time to eighteen months from the current three to five years by 1987. He came up with the slogan "18 by 87." Mac demurred and suggested the eighteen-month goal be set for 1984, a reelection year for President Reagan. After a detailed briefing that showed how the goal could not be reached that quickly without damaging the quality of the reviews and the operation of the office, Mac signed on to "18 by 87" and lobbied Congress to get key Democrats to support it.

The 1987 deadline was not met. After Mossinghoff resigned in 1985, the budget for the Commerce Department was cut, so it took an additional two years. The goal of eighteen months turn-around time was reached in 1989, providing the best patent application response time in modern times, before or since.

With a mandate to improve patent operations, the Reagan administration also followed through on a proposal from the Carter administration to create a special patent appeals court in the early spring of 1982. This was called the Court of Appeals for the Federal Circuit, and it would hear all patent cases and create uniformity and certainty in the appeals process. Before creation of this special court, different judges in different circuits interpreted the laws on patents and trademarks in different ways, creating a tremendous amount of confusion. Business favors consistency, and the new court cleared away a great deal of the confusion of contradictory decisions from different courts.

Each year Mossinghoff delivered a state of the Patent and Trademark Office address to the American Bar Association lawyers who specialized in patents, trademarks, and copyright law. In his final address to them in August 1984, he hailed Mac's role in the transformation of the office. "These accomplishments would not have been possible without the strong and continuing support of Secretary Malcolm Baldrige," he said. "From the very start of this Administration, he has been determined to bring about significant and lasting improvements in the Patent and Trademark Office and in the protection of intellectual property worldwide. On many occasions his personal involvement has been indispensable in overcoming bureaucratic obstacles and in resolving political issues."

Another problem Mac addressed was counterfeiting. The explosion of overseas manufacturing concerns fed piracy activities that were draining dollars from the United States. The problem centered in Asia, particularly Taiwan and South Korea. At that time, the Commerce Department estimated that counterfeiting by foreign manufacturers cost legitimate U.S. companies between $8 billion and $20 billion in lost sales of both products and technologies. The counterfeited items were eclectic, ranging from Cabbage Patch dolls that enjoyed raging popularity at the time to designer blue jeans, Hollywood movies, and American music. In April 1986, Mac announced a crackdown. "People are dancing all over the world to counterfeit U.S. tapes—fast dancing and slow dancing," said Mac. Again, the Reagan administration wanted trading partners to take responsibility for illegal activities occurring within their own borders. Using the stick of tariff concessions, Mac challenged countries to take steps to protect American patents, copyrights, and trademarks. A country that condoned counterfeiting or pirating would lose trade preferences.

Better management of the Department led to results. The personal computer industry was just beginning to evolve, but Mac and others recognized that computers would eventually change the way everyone did business. In April 1985, Mac signed an agreement between the government and computer industry officials that help set international standards that would allow computers made by different companies to communicate with one another. Without these sorts of agreements, a Mac computer made by Apple would not be able to communicate with computers using the Windows software developed by Microsoft.

Satellite communications was another fledgling industry at that time. During the Kennedy administration, Congress created the Communications Satellite Corporation (COMSAT), a publically funded corporation charged with developing a commercial satellite system in the United States. At that time, satellites were yet another symbol of the Cold War between the United States and the Soviet Union. The Soviets shocked Americans when they sent *Sputnik I*, the first artificial Earth satellite, into orbit in 1957. *Sputnik* triggered a space war between the two countries. At the same time, it was not unusual for the government to provide the seed money and the initiative to promising new industries. Satellites were a far more efficient way of transmitting wireless signals throughout the country and the world than a telegram carried between continents via undersea cables. Long before the Internet and widespread use of cell phones, the ease of transmitting a voice or image via a satellite in space held great appeal, particularly in remote areas where construction of telephone or electrical poles was impractical or impossible. Within two years of the creation of COMSAT, the United States and allies created an international counterpart called the International Telecommunications Satellite Consortium (Intelsat). This was another area where the dip-

lomats at the State Department did not always agree with the
Commerce Department, according to David Markey, then
the head of the National Telecommunications Information
Administration (NTIA), the agency charged with operating telecommunications and information systems for the
Commerce Department. In the 1980s, governments were the
only ones with pockets deep enough to afford the extraordinary costs of building and delivering satellites into orbit.
Satellites were dependent upon rocket technology, then in
the domain of the military. But Mac recognized satellites
were a potential growth area for business and wanted to ease
the way for private business to compete and eventually take
over the industry. State Department officials preferred the
status quo, because the status quo eased good relationships
with foreign nations. In fact, State Department diplomats so
often questioned whether the Commerce Department had
the authority to make decisions in this area that Mac carried
with him a copy of Executive Order 12046, the Carter administration document that gave Commerce the responsibility
and control over satellite technology. Markey says Mac pulled
out a copy of the order to brandish to State Department officials so often that his copy became worn and dog-eared from
use. Mac often exhorted Markey to be more aggressive and
tougher in his dealings with the State Department.

Mac did not shy away from disputes involving complicated business matters. One prickly issue arose when
Hollywood producers successfully lobbied President Reagan
to support their position on a long-standing dispute over distribution and profits of network television show reruns. The
dispute over who would syndicate and profit from prime-time
television shows had been raging between the major television networks and Hollywood producers for decades. The
networks paid Hollywood production companies to produce
their shows, but often the payment did not cover production

costs. Producers gambled that their shows would become hits and generate profits in reruns or syndication.

In the earliest years of television, the three major networks, ABC, CBS, and NBC, had no competition, because cable television did not yet exist. Essentially they held a monopoly. The TV networks had become both powerful and profitable as television quickly became popular with Americans during the 1950s and 1960s. In the 1970s, an agreement had been negotiated between the government and the networks, awarding the profits from syndication to the producers.

By the time Reagan took office, the competitive situation for the networks was beginning to change. Cable TV companies, including future powerhouses like Home Box Office (HBO), were beginning operations, and network executives recognized that soon they would be facing a great deal of competition for viewers. Reagan's stance favoring the deregulation of business prompted his appointees at the Federal Communications Commission (the FCC) to revisit syndication rules and recommend they be canceled and allow the networks to control all the profits from their shows, even in reruns. Hollywood producers were opposed to any change, arguing that syndication profits allowed them to take chances on new, more creative shows. They said that the networks were profitable enough without the syndication fees, which often provided the only profit the producers would ever realize.

This control over syndication of sales had implications for the future of television programming quality as well as hundreds of millions of dollars in future profits. The Hollywood producers pulled out all the stops against the FCC proposal in order to keep the syndication profit rules intact. At one point, Mac got on a flight to Paris and discovered that Jack Valenti, then the president of the Motion Picture

Association of America, just happened to be sitting next to him. It was clearly no coincidence. Valenti was a relentless advocate for the movie industry. Mac told Markey that Valenti lobbied him for the entire flight across the Atlantic.

The NTIA, the telecommunications agency, had long been on record supporting the FCC's position. In their view, this rule change was part of a trend toward deregulation of various industries and consistent with Reagan's view that government should stay out of private business. Mac agreed with this approach. This hands-off attitude was a fundamental tenet of Reaganomics. There was a great deal of debate during the first Reagan term over whether the United States should adopt an industrial policy in response to the decline of manufacturing in the United States. This issue gives insight into the attitude toward deregulation and the government's relationship with private business. In an article he wrote, Mac was quite firm on the subject: "Our economic problems have usually stemmed from burdens on the free market, such as high interest rates, inflation, heavy taxes and over-regulation. Therefore, we should not turn to a national industrial policy that involves increased government intervention into the economy."

An argument could be made that the syndication rule was outdated because it had been implemented at a time television was the new kid on the block in entertainment, competing with the powerful, well-established movie studios. But once the president got involved at the behest of his longtime Hollywood friends, any commitment to policy consistency went out the window, and everything changed. Mac called Markey back on a red-eye flight from out of town to accompany him to the White House to brief the president. Reagan listened to the argument and made no comment. Markey heard nothing else until the night before a congressional hearing on the issue, when Mac's office notified Markey that he needed to go with Mac to another White House meeting on the issue. This time, Presidential Counselor Ed Meese told them that the Department had to change its position and oppose the FCC decision to abolish those rules preserving syndication profits for the production companies. Markey anticipated this reversal because of Reagan's personal interest in the well-being of Hollywood. As a joke, he brought along a wind-up toy kangaroo. He wound it up, and the toy did back flips over and over again, much to everyone's amusement.

Mac did not feel strongly about the issue. It was a battle he did not care to fight. There were times when he disagreed with President Reagan, but this issue was not one he felt strongly enough to challenge. Mac believed in the chain of command, and he respected the presidency as well as Reagan personally. It is issues like this one that showed that Mac was no ideologue. Markey had to explain the reversal to the members of Congress the next day, and he simply said that he worked for the president and was following the president's lead. In any case, ten years later, several years after Reagan had left office, the rules on syndication were changed.

Mac felt more strongly about the breakup of AT&T, the telephone monopoly, but it was an issue that was out of his hands. The antitrust division of the Justice Department had brought a lawsuit against AT&T in 1974. The company worked out a settlement in 1982 when it recognized that the government had the upper hand. In their view, it was more prudent to cut a deal in advance of a court order that may have imposed a far harsher remedy on them. Mac privately believed the breakup was a mistake, because AT&T ran an extremely efficient operation. AT&T provided all long-distance telephone service in the country and a majority of the local service. It was a massive operation that included Western Electric, the company that manufactured all of the telephone equipment for the nation, with a million employees. Efficiency in telephone service means a great deal to business. It is difficult to do business if the telephone, then a major means of communication, is often out of service. Of course, the efficiency came with a price. There was little choice in equipment or options. AT&T had the ability to produce wireless telephones years before cellular telephones became ubiquitous but chose not to produce them because company executives did not think people would want a wireless telephone.

Mac believed business had a responsibility to operate with efficiency and to invest in research and development. He once told the Senate Finance Committee, which was considering creating incentives for the high-technology sector, that the government did a lousy job of interfering in the private market.

"Trying to predict winners and channeling investment funds would be a mistake," he said. "Interventionist government policies have not worked in the past and there is no reason to believe we can make them work now. It is the private sector's and not the government's responsibility to fund the commercialization of new products and processes. The government's role is to remove barriers and create a conducive environment."

While business leaders did not care to be subject to the stern lectures Mac could deliver on management deficiencies, they knew they had a friend in Mac Baldrige. He often acted as a bridge between interests. "Mac was one of those guys who knew you had to talk to both customers and suppliers," said Bruce Smart, who served as Mac's second Under Secretary of Trade. In business, Mac had followed this practice of consulting with all parties involved, and he maintained it in government, consulting widely with members of Congress, business executives, other cabinet secretaries, and his own career employees.

Roger B. Smith, the chairman of General Motors, wrote a note to Mac toward the end of 1984: "It is certainly good to be able to talk with you when we have a serious problem and get the kind of response you gave last week. Your willingness to help at a critical point is a good example of why the Commerce Department has the excellent reputation it now enjoys with the business community."

9

PLAIN ENGLISH WITH A SIDE OF HUMOR

M AC MAJORED IN ENGLISH AT YALE AND WROTE HIS senior thesis on the works of Geoffrey Chaucer, one of the greatest English poets of the Middle Ages. Until Chaucer's time, well-educated Englishmen read literature in Latin or French. Chaucer, however, wrote in English and made spoken English, the popular vernacular, legitimate for use in English literature. This made poetry more accessible to the English people. Like Chaucer, Mac believed language should be clear and succinct. Cowboys, he often noted, spoke little, but what they did say mattered. He followed this practice from college all the way through his business and government careers. At his confirmation hearing on January 6, 1981, he was invited by the chairman of the Senate Committee on Commerce, Science, and Transportation to make any opening remarks he wished. He replied with a single sentence: "If I am confirmed, I know how to work hard, and I would be a good Secretary of Commerce."

A plaque with his favorite cowboy saying hung in the family kitchen in Woodbury. It said:

> *Be careful of the words you speak*
> *Keep them soft and sweet*
> *You never know from day to day*
> *Which ones you'll have to eat.*

Mac recoiled against bureaucratic language that deflected, obscured, and confused meaning or intent. He insisted on language that enlightened and informed. This was a passionate cause throughout his life. Bureaucratic language can be found in all professions, and he was convinced that inflated words and phrases were a smokescreen either to hide deficiencies in the writer's ideas or to allow the writer to shirk responsibility and avoid taking a position. At Scovill, he required his employees to use plain English in business correspondence. He often expressed frustration if a letter did not tell him clearly whether the writer had said yes or no. In Mac's view, if a constituent or customer asked a question, he or she deserved an answer. Mac wanted clarity in his letters and indeed in all correspondence and writing, ranging from internal staff memos to messages to the president. He also deliberately spoke in a very quiet voice. This caused his audience to lean in and listen more intently to hear him. He was convinced that people heard him better if they had to make an effort to listen and were not assaulted with loud words.

Mac's drive to bring plain English to the government was perceived by some as a David and Goliath struggle against the implacable bureaucracy, or like Don Quixote, tilting at windmills. Mac took on decades of gobbledygook and obfuscation. Jack Anderson, the formidable investigative reporter whose syndicated column was required reading in Washington, wrote, "A true revolutionary has surfaced in the Reagan administration in the unlikely person of Commerce Secretary Malcolm Baldrige. He has declared war on wordiness, clichés, government jargon and the kind of bafflegab so beloved by Washington bureaucrats." An editorial in the *Naugatuck Daily News* in Connecticut, with the headline "Congratulations, Mac!" said, "The use of jargon has become a part of our way of life, causing confusion, misunderstandings, delays and frustration. So our hats go off to Malcolm Baldrige for taking this step towards controlling the pollution of our mother tongue."

Plain English was also a big hit with reporters. Mac often cited *The Elements of Style* by Strunk and White as a bible for the correct usage. For generations, first-year English majors have been assigned "The Little Book" as required reading. It was initially drafted and self-published in 1918 by William Strunk Jr., an English professor at Cornell. One of his students, the writer E. B. White, a longtime *New Yorker* magazine staff member and the author of the children's classic *Charlotte's Web*, revised the book in 1959 for the college market. "The Little Book" is a pithy ode to simplicity and basic English rules. In the days before a Google search was a gleam in the eye, writers, including many newspaper reporters and editors, kept a dictionary, a thesaurus, and *The Elements of Style* within easy reach.

Mac drafted a memo on use of plain English at Scovill for his employees, and a variation of this memo was introduced at Commerce. The three-page directive called "Secretary's Writing Style" begins: "Clarity and brevity are the key factors when preparing correspondence for the Secretary or Deputy Secretary. The Secretary wants short sentences and short words, with emphasis on *plain English*. Use no more words than effective expression requires."

The memo was very specific. It prohibited the use of nouns or adjectives as verbs, such as "to impact, to interface, or it obsoletes." It ruled out any affected or imprecise words, including "*alternatives, orient, dialogue, effectuated, facilitate, input* and *output.*" The memo said that *–ize* words such as *finalize, maximize,* and *prioritize* should no longer be used. His pet peeves were listed, and their use forbidden, including "*in terms of, in the near future, needless to say, positive feedback* and *contingent upon.*" He waged total war on redundancies, including "*enclosed herewith, end result, future plans, important essentials, untimely death, new initiatives, personally reviewed* and *serious crisis.*"

To make everything crystal clear and pay homage to his inspiration, the memo ends with one of the most famous passages from *The Elements of Style*:

> Vigorous writing is concise. A sentence should contain no unnecessary words, a paragraph no unnecessary sentences, for the same reason that a drawing should have no unnecessary lines and a machine no unnecessary parts. This requires not that the writer make all his sentences short, or that he avoid all detail and treat his subjects only in outline, but that he make every word tell.

The final sentence of the memo reads: "Secretary Baldrige says, 'In short, halfway between Ernest Hemingway and Zane Grey with *no bureaucratese.*'" When the memo was first circulated, Mac claimed, "You couldn't find a copy of Zane Grey within 20 blocks of the Commerce Department because employees bought them all."

Mac was serious about this directive. More than one senior Commerce employee resisted the idea of being told how to write, and more than a few were openly disdainful. But Mac held a mass meeting for managers in the Commerce Department auditorium to make a personal appeal for the use of plain English. He was humble, soft spoken, and asked them to do it for him.

He hired Dr. Thomas Murawski, a retired air force lieutenant colonel, who had taught English to military cadets, to run writing seminars for Commerce Department employees. Murawski was scheduled to spend a few days at the Department, holding classes in the morning and the afternoon. His first morning class was poorly attended. The Commerce auditorium, which held a few thousand people, was not even half full. That afternoon's session, though, was packed to capacity, with standing room only. Why? Because Murawski was not only an expert in plain language, he was funny and entertaining, making the classes not just easy to take but good for laughs.

Dr. Murawski had requested, weeks before he came to Commerce, examples of Commerce writing. The Department submitted letters and memos for his review. At his classes, he would show those letters or memos on an overhead projector, revealing each document (but not their authors) to the entire auditorium. He then would edit the document on the screen, poking fun as he went along at the obvious examples of obfuscation, inflation, or incorrect use of words and phrases. The audience erupted in laughter when they saw how badly the memos and letters were written and how so many never answered the question asked. He got his points across. During the lunch break, word around the building spread like wildfire about the hilarity generated by his session, so every class that week was packed. He was so popular that other cabinet departments brought him in to teach their employees. This effort made good copy for reporters and editorial writers who were amused by the improbability of forcing bureaucrats to use simple, declarative sentences. Mac's efforts resulted in hundreds of news features, columns, and editorials across the country, mostly praising his crusade.

Department employees eventually took pride in this directive in a way that demonstrates the unusual bond between the Secretary and the thousands of people who worked for him. While Mac demanded a great deal from the government workers in his Department, he also looked out for them. The Commerce Department is located on one of the most prominent corners of downtown Washington, the Federal Triangle, just blocks from the White House, and next to the famous Washington Mall that stretches a mile from the Lincoln Monument all the way to the steps of the Capitol. The National Park Service launched a summer series of public concerts on the Ellipse in 1976 to entertain the tourists who were waiting to visit the White House. The concerts, designed to entertain up to ten thousand visitors, featured marching bands from high schools all over the country, playing at 10 a.m. and 12:30 p.m. in a band shell that faced the Commerce Department. The music, with amplification provided by a National Park Service sound system, reverberated in the large, cavernous rooms of the entire side of the Commerce Department that faces the Ellipse. The noise was so loud that Mac could not have a conversation with trade ministers or anyone else in his office. Thousands of Commerce Department employees were disturbed by the noise. Mac complained every summer, and by the third year, the National Park Service removed the speakers and seventy-six of the eighty-five bands scheduled to travel to Washington for the concerts canceled. The Park Service likely leaked the story to the media. The uproar was immediate. In a memo to Mac, his press secretary, B. Jay Cooper, reported that he had fielded more than forty calls from the media, including every major broadcast network. This took place at the end of July 1983, when most of official Washington is either on vacation or packing to head out of town for the steamiest month of the year. Mac had never asked that the concerts stop, only that the volume be reduced. The controversy literally blew over within days, but his employees who were distracted by the thunderous marching bands during their work day never forgot that their boss was willing to risk public criticism to improve their working conditions.

The stories about language are legion. Gerry McKiernan once received a request from Mac for details about a piece of legislation pending on Capitol Hill. Gerry drafted a summary of the bill and walked into Mac's office, saying, "Here is a small summary that synopsizes it for you." When Mac heard the word *synopsize* on top of the redundant *small summary*, he gave Gerry "that look," a distinctive expression that conveyed horror, dismay, and disapproval with one glance. Gerry immediately realized his error, backtracked, and blurted that he had "a summary, only a summary." When he returned to his office, he looked up the word *synopsize* and found it in the dictionary. He copied the page from the dictionary and went back to Mac's office. He slid it across the desk and said, "So you see, sir, it is a word." Mac held his folded reading glasses up to his eyes, as he often did, not taking the time to open them and put them on, to peer through the lenses. He silently read the dictionary definition, put the glasses down, looked up at Gerry, and said, "Shouldn't be."

Eugene Lawson, a senior trade official, told Midge about a time at the conclusion of the first Joint Commission meeting with the Chinese when Mac, Lawson, the U.S. Ambassador to China, and a few others gathered to prepare for a press conference. Mac asked Lawson what he thought he should say about export controls. Lawson said, "I always use the phrase that the scale, scope and speed of our exports has greatly changed in the last year." Lawson was extremely pleased with his alliteration and was unprepared when Mac looked straight at him and said, "That is really awful! Try again!" Mac's candid remark had all of them, including Lawson, convulsed in laughter for the next five minutes.

Lionel Olmer had been an English major at the University of Connecticut, so he had his own strong views about literature and what constituted good writing. He and Mac once disagreed about the quality of a magazine article written by the English playwright John Osborne, who tended to write in very long sentences, completely at odds with Mac's preference for the short, almost staccato phrasing of an Ernest Hemingway or Zane Grey.

"I told him, you're not going to like this article but this guy writes beautifully," remembered Olmer. Mac often used his pack of Marlboro cigarettes as a prop. It gave him time to think. He kept his cigarettes in his back pocket, crushing the pack every time he sat down. He would pull out the crumbled package, and stand in a particular way dictated by his fused spine that recalled the lopsided posture of a cowboy at rest on the range. Then he would languidly pull out a cigarette, stick it in his mouth, and spit out a tiny bit of tobacco before speaking. After Lionel's pronouncement on the excellence of John Osborne's prose, Mac pulled out a cigarette, spat out a bit of tobacco, and drawled, "Bullshit. He doesn't write the way I want."

Pat Corken ran the office called Executive Secretariat, which handled all the correspondence and paperwork for the Secretary of Commerce. She was a career government employee who got the top job from Mac, even though a political appointee always held the position. She remembered another time the staff decided to have some fun with the directive that gender-specific language be eliminated where possible. Instead of *workman*, the term should be *worker*, *chairperson* instead of *chairman*, *reporter* instead of *newsman*, *police officer* instead of *policeman*. In the middle of the list of examples, the staff inserted: "Do not use *cowboy* or *cowgirl*, use *cow person*." His assistant took the doctored memo into him. When he spotted the change, he roared and jumped to his feet. As he thundered out of his office, Pat stood there to assure him, "Sir, it is a joke!" She went on, "Once he calmed down, he was fine." There were limits to his mandate as well. There were employees at the National Oceanic and Atmospheric Administration (NOAA) who would follow a directive right over a cliff. One day an employee decided to substitute the word *fisher* for *fisherman*. This was a step too far for Mac, who ordered them to keep *fisherman*.

Pat said that Mac felt so strongly about using plain English that he would walk a letter with a single offensive item from his office down the hall to her office to point it out and ask that it be fixed. He refused to sign any letter with any violation of the plain English edict or a breach of grammar or punctuation. There were times when a midlevel bureaucrat insisted upon writing a letter his way instead of the Secretary's way. If the letter was going out with Mac's signature, it was always caught by the Secretary and sent back to the author for correction, she said.

His penchant for precision in language was not limited to the written word. When he was named the Professional Rodeo Cowboy Association "Man of the Year," the Associated Press called his spokesman seeking a comment. Mac was at a meeting and not available to approve a quote, so the spokesman told the reporter, on deadline and wanting to move the story onto the wire as soon as possible, that Mac was "thrilled" to be named. When the story hit the wire, the spokesman put the story on Mac's desk so he would see it on his return, assuming he would be "thrilled" that the wire wrote a story about the honor that meant a great deal to him. Mac returned, read the story, and, still looking intently at the article in his hand, walked into his spokesman's office, looked up, said, "I don't get 'thrilled,'" and walked out. From then on he was never "thrilled" in response to anything, but he was "proud" or "honored" and sometimes just "pleased."

Because the interest in simple English became something of a crusade, Mac attracted an enthusiastic following among writers whose craft requires succinct clarity. His head of public affairs had a sign hanging in his office with a framed quotation from H. G. Wells, as a message to his staff: "No passion on earth, neither love nor hate, is equal to the passion to alter someone else's draft." An Association of Government Public Affairs employee asked him to write about his interest for their newsletter. He wrote: "One's goal in communications should be to use lean language that gets the meaning across directly. I believed that strongly before I came to Washington and I believe it even more strongly today. Writing and speaking styles tell a great deal about individuals. A pretentious style usually indicates an urge to sound important or a protective mechanism to fog up recommendations to diminish accountability. This is the most common problem we encounter in government writing. Unfortunately, neither of those is what one is paid to do."

The Unicorn Hunters at Lake Superior State College in Sault Ste. Marie, Michigan, a group of students with a deep affection for correct language usage, issued lists each year to banish words and phrases that were overused, misused, or just considered useless. Mac's campaign came to their attention. In 1982, the Unicorn Hunters proclaimed Mac the first "Knight Sans Pareil of the Unicorn Quest" and dubbed him Sir Malcolm of Potomac for his plain English campaign.

Ostensibly, Mac's plain English crusade concerned the clarity of the written word. But it was actually much more than that. On a deeper level, it reflected Mac's basic tenets of life: living in truth, taking personal responsibility, having the courage of one's convictions, treating all other human beings with respect and kindness, and using humor to keep a healthy perspective.

A cynic might wonder if Mac's cowboy bearing, focus on plain language, candor, sense of humor, and ability to toss off earthy and quotable remarks was a deliberate public relations strategy, aimed at making him stand out among his peers. It was not a strategy. It was genuine. These characteristics endeared him to reporters, who prize those elements of "good copy," and they contributed to his success in building productive relationships at the White House, within the cabinet and across the political aisle. Journalists saw him as a welcome respite from the uptight, highly controlled obfuscation of Washington. With Mac, communication was easy, open, and relaxed—nothing was forced or false.

Mac had enough self-confidence and status to make good-natured fun of his peers in the cabinet. In the 1980s, the National Press Club, a building in downtown Washington just a block from Commerce, was the premier venue for Washington newsmakers. The office building was filled with news bureaus, with the press club on the top floor, complete with the legendary bar and piano on which the young, beautiful Lauren Bacall languidly posed as President Harry Truman played a tune. If anyone or any cause wanted to get a lot of publicity quickly, their event was scheduled at the National Press Club, with its captive audience of journalists and lobbyists. For one speech in 1981, Mac began his remarks with a riff he had written himself on the psychological aspects of Reagan's famous jelly bean jar. President Reagan was well known for his affection for the candy. He kept a clear container full of jelly beans in the Oval Office and another on the table for cabinet meetings in the Roosevelt Room. A treasured White House gift was a personalized box of jelly jeans from the president. This is what Mac said to open his speech:

You're all familiar with the fact that President Reagan is a jelly bean addict—and that he shares a jar of jelly beans with his Cabinet each time we meet. The jar starts in front of Dave Stockman. There, unfortunately, it also stops dead. The Budget Director is scribbling down numbers—and putting minus signs after them. This demands his total attention. Psychological interpretation: a man whose pleasures lie in long-term numbers, not in short-term gratification.

After the jelly bean jar is stuck in front of Dave for a while, Defense Secretary Caspar Weinberger usually gets impatient. He reaches in front of me to slide the jar down the table. Defense is getting the lion's share of everything this year.

Now the jar goes to the President, who gives a virtuoso performance. If he's gesturing with his right hand, he backhands with his left and extracts a full measure of jelly beans. If his right hand is free, he makes a quick dip into the jar without looking, and comes up with a full measure in that hand. Psychological interpretation: a very secure leader who knows exactly what he wants and gets it.

Vice-President George Bush always goes for the licorice beans, and if none are available he gobbles chocolate ones instead. Psychological interpretation: a man who goes all out for what he wants but will settle for something almost as good if he has to.

Secretary of State Alexander Haig grasps the jar firmly with both hands, peers with great intensity into its depths and searches until he finds two red jelly beans. These he pops into his mouth and there is an audible crunch as he masticates them into oblivion. Interpretation: The man just doesn't like the color red.

He said Energy Secretary James Edwards, a former dentist, never touched the candy jar but turned white at the sight of

Reagan gulping handfuls of jelly beans, doubtless envisioning a future of tooth cavities.

This type of gentle, mocking humor loaded with double entendres was a big hit with reporters who might make similar jokes privately among themselves but rarely heard a Cabinet Secretary engage in such overt teasing of his esteemed colleagues.

In fact, gentle ribbing was a very successful tool that Mac often used, as did his sister Tish—telling the truth that others are thinking but won't state out loud, sometimes in an exaggerated way. He understood that the truth was usually funnier than anything else, and this form of truthful teasing worked for Mac because of his ability to do it with humor and kindness. He never used it in a hurtful way but rather to indicate his underlying appreciation of the person being teased and his acceptance of him or her as a representative of the human condition and all of its foibles. It was a brilliant technique, because Mac got to state the truth as he saw it, amuse people, not hurt anyone's feelings, yet get the point across. He did this in all aspects of his life. Another example: Mac took his family with him whenever possible to the rodeos in which he competed. His express intent with Megan and Molly was to expose them to all aspects of rodeo cowboys at an early age, so they would not run off with one when they were teenagers. One evening in a small California town, the whole family was eating supper with fellow rodeo contestants at a restaurant across the parking lot from the motel where the cowboys stayed. Megan, then sixteen years old, got up from the table and said she was going to bed, prompting a Texan bull rider to jump up and say, "Mac, I'll see her to her room safely," to which Mac replied with a smile, "Sit down, Jim, she's safer out there by herself in the dark than with you."

Another example of his understated humor, exemplifying his healthy perspective on Washington formalities, involved his crumpled cigarettes. Often on Saturday nights, Mac and Midge had to attend formal dinners in Washington. After spending the afternoon sitting in his Western saddle on the soft pack of Marlboros in his back pocket, he would simply transfer the cigarettes from his jeans to his tuxedo pants. After dinner, he would advance a rounded, beat up, practically broken cigarette a third of the way out of the pack. Turning to the well-dressed ladies on either side, he would say quietly in mock formality, "Would you care for an English Oval?"

Mac's sense of humor extended to the things he held dear, such as clear communication. Paul O'Day, the textile expert, decided to make a joke at the Secretary's expense on the day Mac made his personal appeal on writing to the Department employees. O'Day raced back to his office and dictated a mock memo from Mac to department employees about writing quality and included an "example" of his Zane Grey/Ernest Hemingway style of communication.

> To Bill Brock USTR
> Dear Ambassador Brock,
> No.
> (signed) Mac Baldrige, Secretary of Commerce
> P.S. Damn it!

He delivered the mock memo to Mac's office and was told Mac laughed out loud at the parody.

Meg Greenfield, the legendary editorial page editor for the *Washington Post*, interviewed him for a Sunday morning network magazine show once on the subject of language. He sent a thank-you note that said, "Dear Meg, Thanks. Sincerely, Malcolm Baldrige."

10

LEGACY

AT THE END OF JULY IN 1987, MAC HEADED TO THE Brentwood, California, ranch of his friend Jack Roddy for a roping practice. The ranch is located in Contra Costa County, less than an hour drive from San Francisco. Roping with his fellow cowboys had been Mac's favorite pastime for thirty years and was doubtless a welcome break after months of intense work.

It had been a difficult year, beginning with his hospitalization with pneumonia. That July Washington, D.C., was experiencing one of its overheated summer months; the temperature had been in the nineties all week, hitting one hundred degrees on Tuesday. The weather, as always in Washington in the summer, was hot, humid, and unpleasant. The city typically slowed down and emptied out in late July; Congress and the Supreme Court left for recess, and the rest of official Washington took advantage of their absence for vacations of their own.

On Saturday, Mac had borrowed a heeling horse and was sitting on him at the side of the arena, waiting his turn to practice with his heading partner. No one will ever know what precisely went wrong, but the horse reared and went over backward, trapping Mac underneath it. A helicopter rushed him to John Muir Hospital in Walnut Creek, but there was little the doctors could do. His internal injuries were massive. He died on the operating table on Saturday, July 25, 1987. He was sixty-four years old.

By its nature, an accidental death is shocking. There is no warning, no way to anticipate, prepare, or brace for the loss. Back in Washington, his staff members were running errands and preparing for their own summer vacations that Saturday. When Helen Robbins, his loyal executive assistant, got the phone call telling her the boss had died, her daughter remembers that Helen wailed in grief, a visceral guttural cry of pain. Helen, though, wasted no time in accomplishing a more immediate task: stopping Midge from leaving for California to be with Mac. Midge was on a commercial flight already on the runway, and thanks to Helen's formidable abilities, the plane returned to the gate to let Midge off.

The rituals that follow the death of a prominent man took place. On Wednesday, President Reagan delivered the eulogy at a memorial service at the National Cathedral, which was filled to capacity with standing room only. The ceremony took thirty minutes, in keeping with Mac's fondness for brevity. Jack Danforth, a U.S. senator from Missouri and an ordained Episcopal priest, presided over the service, at Midge's request. The president was the sole eulogist, and his tribute was perfect. The president said that Mac embodied the best of the American spirit, and he recalled that Mac had a standing order to immediately put through phone calls from only two sources: President Reagan or any cowboy who wanted to talk to him. The president remarked on Mac's generous democratic nature. "He treated everyone with the same courtesy and respect, from his driver to the president. Despite his many remarkable successes, worldly success was not the way he measured people . . . honesty, courage, industry and humility, these were his yardsticks."

In a personal letter to Midge dated two days after Mac's death, Reagan told her that he and Nancy felt "devastated" by Mac's passing. "I think you know pretty well by now that Mac was my idea of a perfect public servant," he wrote. "I deeply valued his realism, his passion for facts, his wide-ranging insight into the world economy, and—above all—his love for this nation and its people . . . Mac was my friend, and I'll be forever proud to say I was one of his."

The president provided a government plane to fly Mac's body back to Connecticut. The flag-draped casket, accompanied by an honor guard, arrived at the small local airport where his family waited. The next day, after a funeral in the North Congregational Church in Woodbury, Mac was laid to rest at the rural cemetery near the family home. Although there were hundreds in attendance, with many more listening from outside the church, the funeral was smaller and more intimate than the solemn event at the National Cathedral.

Vice President George H. W. Bush kept some of his eulogy light, commenting that Mac's recent jogging efforts were akin to "watching grass grow." Then struggling with his personal grief, tears dropping on his copy of the remarks he prepared, he honored his longtime friend. "This honest man was indeed the noblest work of God," he said in the quiet of the 171-year-old Congregational Church. "I loved him." Nor was there a dry eye during the recessional, as the casket was carried from the church while the organist played an ethereal version of "Home on the Range." Bush sent Midge a hand-written note from *Air Force II* on his way to Iowa the next day that said, "You'll never know how truly honored I was when you asked me to say a few words at Mac's funeral . . . I really did love the guy." He sent her the hand-edited copy of his eulogy and apologized for the tear stains on the paper.

Senator Alan K. Simpson, another man of the West, delivered the quintessential cliché that seemed so perfect at that moment. "One of the finest things you can say about a cowboy is that he died with his boots on," he said. "That was Mac. And now we must give him up."

Giving up a man who had seemed so vibrant and present just days before was not easy. As the funeral took place in Woodbury, another memorial service was under way at the Commerce Department in Washington. Thousands of employees turned out to honor their boss. Career bureaucrats, many named to their top jobs by Mac, spoke of how much they appreciated his decency; how grateful they were for being treated with respect and dignity; and how much his leadership meant to the department, its reputation, and to each of them in a deeply personal way. Mac had told whoever would listen, including titans of industry who often held public employees in contempt, that the career employees at the Department of Commerce could hold their own with the best in the private sector. No one was brighter, worked harder, or exhibited more integrity, he said. He meant every word, and the career employees knew it. Their gratitude was genuine. A young black driver from the motor pool read a personal message from Wesley Goad, Mac's driver, who was attending the funeral in Woodbury that day. Wes wrote that Mac was more like a brother than boss. The gathering also received a brief message from Midge. She wrote a note telling them that Mac had died happy, doing what he loved, a comforting thought from the bereft widow who would never get over the loss of her husband of thirty-six years and confessed to friends, in letters she wrote months later, that she still felt befogged and bewildered.

After Mac's death, Midge received many condolence letters. Few were as moving as the three-page letter she received from Hajime Tamura, the minister of International Trade and Industry for Japan. Writing the letter four days after Mac's death, he told her that he was still in a state of disbelief. He told her that Mac had written him a poem that Mac described as his attempt at a Japanese haiku. The poem read.

> *Tamura-san has come,*
> *He hasn't come unnoticed,*
> *He goes, his words stay.*

Tamura recalled that they had last met in mid-July in Washington, just before Mac's death. "For me," he wrote, "it was a most depressing trip. I was in Washington to deal with problems connected with the Toshiba Machine affair, which threatened to cause serious harm to Japan's relations with the United States." Toshiba Machine, a subsidiary of the third largest electronics firm in Japan, had sold $17 million worth of milling equipment to the Soviet Union. This equipment made the Soviet submarines ten times more difficult for U.S. Navy vessels to hear. This disclosure created an uproar on Capitol Hill. Nine members of Congress held a press conference on July 2, 1987, and smashed a small Toshiba radio with sledgehammers to demonstrate their anger. The issue crystallized the fear that the United States was losing its technological edge and possibly the long Cold War with the Soviet Union. Later that month, by 98 percent of the votes, the Senate amended a trade bill to impose a five-year embargo on Toshiba imports to the United States. Emotions were running high.

In his letter, Tamura said that Mac took the tension out of their encounter. "Mr. Baldrige gave me a warm reception that considerably lightened my spirits. We concluded what could be called the 'Baldrige-Tamura Agreement' to work together to prevent any further violations of COCOM [the coordinating committee for multinational export controls]. By skillfully explaining the 'agreement' to the newspapers, Mr. Baldrige did a great deal for my reputation." The *Washington Post*, for instance, reported that "Japanese assurances satisfy Baldrige." "At the time I left for Washington," he wrote, "I had my letter of resignation in my pocket, so completely was I prepared for what I viewed as the inevitable. But with the press coverage made possible by Mac's friendship, I was somehow able to escape that predicament. I wish above all that I could stand before him now and say: Mac, let me call you by your first name. Let me thank you as you deserve to be thanked. To the end of my days, I shall never forget the friendship you showed me."

Tamura told Midge that he wept when he heard of Mac's death. He wrote, "The tears I shed were not only for an important friend of my country, now lost to it, but for my own friend, close and irreplaceable. As a fitting remembrance to him, I shall redouble my efforts to more fully understand his country, the United States of America." For an official from a country where form, saving face, manners, and self-control are so important, it was an extraordinarily personal and revealing letter.

Ritual can provide great comfort to the bereaved, or at least help them get through the first painful days and weeks after a death. In Mac's case, there was a palpable sense that a memorial service or a funeral was insufficient. He died at the culmination of his tenure as Commerce Secretary, but he was not yet finished. President Reagan presented him with the Presidential Medal of Freedom posthumously on October 17,

1988. The citation read: "Cowboy, business executive, political activist, Cabinet Secretary—Mac Baldrige was all of these and more. To every task and role, he brought the strength of his integrity and the power of his vision. In serving his country, he became an architect of our international economic policy. And yet, though he moved with Presidents, Prime Ministers, and Kings, he was always happiest with the kind of straight talking cowboys who elected him to the Cowboy Hall of Fame. Malcolm Baldrige had uncommon accomplishments and character. He was a true embodiment of the American spirit."

Within weeks of Mac's death, however, a lasting memorial that built upon his legacy began to take form. If Mac Baldrige stood for anything, he stood for excellence and quality. He believed firmly that American business could compete with anyone and had been telling business leaders for years that neglect of business fundamentals came with a dire price. He was not the only person who worried about national competitiveness. The rise of Japan troubled many. Mat Heyman, a longtime official at Commerce, remembers that the concern had been mounting. "No one felt comfortable having the United States be second best to Japan or any other country. Germany and Japan were becoming much stronger in manufacturing and they were advancing," he said. President Reagan had established the President's Commission on Industrial Competitiveness in June 1983 to address this issue and recommend ways in which the private sector could better compete throughout the world. By the time Mac died, the concern was widespread. On June 8, 1987, an article in *BusinessWeek*, an influential magazine, reported, "For U.S. industry, the message is clear. Get better or get beaten."

Awards are not always meaningful. Organizations sometimes present honors to wealthy individuals or government officials with the ulterior motive of securing a big donation or some governmental largesse. The idea of a government agency presenting an award to business to recognize excellence and quality was initially laughable. Government was not well regarded by the business community at that time. There was skepticism about the idea that a government agency had the expertise or credibility to tell the private sector how to succeed. But the idea of a special government award, encouraging the business community to systematically improve its game and to share those experiences with one another, had worked well in Japan; their business honor was named after the revered American statistician and business analyst W. Edwards Deming, whose teachings Mac had so admired.

Almost a year before Mac died, Congressman Don Fuqua, a Florida Democrat who was then serving his final year in the U.S. House, introduced legislation to create a national quality improvement award. The goal was to encourage U.S. business and industry to take steps to improve the quality of their goods and services. This legislation reflected Mac's philosophy and the teachings of Deming, whose guidance had been so influential in Japan in the postwar years. The proposal languished, but the following year, Congressman Doug Walgren, a Pennsylvania Democrat, reintroduced the bill and Senator Bob Graham, a Florida Democrat, sponsored a Senate version. The bill passed the U.S. House in early June 1987 and went to the Senate, where nothing happened for the next six weeks.

In a history of the award, Curt Reimann, the first director of the Baldrige program, who was then working at the Commerce Department's National Bureau of Standards (since 1989 known as NIST, the National Institute of Science and Technology), said that Mac's death put new energy behind the legislation. President Reagan liked the idea of naming the award for Mac as a way to honor his friend. Mac had many friends on Capitol Hill, both Democrats and Republicans, and they, too, wanted to honor his memory.

There was probably little that government could do to change the way industrial titans ran their businesses, but this small bill showed that Congress was concerned.

Reimann said, "There was pent-up feeling that something needed to be done about national competitiveness and quality problems. Then, this terrible accident suddenly created a vehicle that people could rally around. Those kinds of confluences are very rare. It was an accident of circumstances." An official history of the program recounts that the Senate Committee on Commerce, Science, and Transportation renamed the bill in Mac's honor three days after his death. The bill passed the Senate, and the House agreed to the name change. On August 20, 1987, less than a month after Mac's death, President Reagan signed the Malcolm Baldrige National Quality Improvement Act of 1987 into law.

It proved to be a living memorial that exists to this day. The Malcolm Baldrige National Quality Award is a highly sought-after prize by businesses of all sizes, nonprofits, and schools. The award sets specific criteria for measuring quality management. The evaluation criteria consider the qualities of leadership, strategic quality planning, information management, human resources, and process management. The prize recognizes organizations that follow processes that nurture smart management, resulting in the production of high-quality services and products. In the criteria, the experience of the customer is as important as technical standards. Competing for the award, and adhering to the specific criteria and standards of the award, produce positive results for the competitors, even for those who do not win. The award application process is designed to ensure that winners actually deserve the award, and many corporations invest a great deal of time and money into applying, knowing that the process alone will improve their processes and operations.

Those who established the criteria decided to focus attention and publicity on the winners and their performance, creating an additional incentive for businesses to compete for the prize. Heyman said that type of emphasis and focus gave the program credibility and value to the business community.

President Reagan launched the Baldrige program at the White House on March 31, 1988. C. William Verity Jr., the longtime steel executive whom Reagan named Secretary of Commerce to replace Mac, described the award as "America's Nobel Prize for quality." The first recipients were announced on November 14, 1988, at a ceremony at the White House.

It is difficult to quantify a legacy. The Commerce Department's reputation waxed and waned after Mac's time, although the career employees still alive today insist that Mac set a standard to which his successors may have aspired but which they rarely achieved. With the benefit of hindsight, it is clear that part of Mac's legacy was the effect he had on others, particularly those who worked at the Department of Commerce. He instilled pride at the Commerce Department. Mac once described his first day on the job as Secretary. Walking into the big, gray building, he passed a booth where two security guards sat behind a desk. He said they were slumped down, and neither even looked up when he passed by. When he inquired about the reason for this dismal greeting, he was told that the security guards simply reflected the quality of people available for lowly positions in the government. Mac was appalled. At the time, he said, "That can pull my cork just about as much as anything."

So he called the security and building receptionist employees to a meeting at his office. This had never happened before, and the employees, among the lowest paid and least prestigious in the department, were stunned. Many were frightened, convinced that they were about to lose their jobs. With no intention of firing anyone that day, Mac spoke to them in a collegial way.

"You know the foreign trade ministers who are responsible for coming up with American exports, and the Congressmen and Senators, and the businessmen who create jobs, come in here and you are the first people they see," he told them. "We depend on you. We need you to get spruced up and be alert and be helpful. And above all, when it gets to be about 5 o'clock in the evening and you are tired, be just as cheerful and helpful as you were at 8 o'clock in the morning." Mac only needed to say it once.

Kay Bulow, who ran administration at Commerce, remembers that his leadership and management style made the department one of the best places to work in Washington during his time in office. The insiders understood the effect that good management had on the operation of the agency. *Government Executive,* a monthly magazine based in Washington covering the business of government for senior government executives and managers, presented its second annual Award for Managerial Excellence in Government to Mac in 1984. The cover of the magazine featured a photograph taken in the Oval Office. Mac stood in the middle, smiling and holding the wooden plaque. Ed Meese, the president's counselor who had won the first award the previous year, stood to his left. President Reagan stood on the right smiling broadly at his Commerce Secretary, looking for all the world like a proud parent.

Mac also left behind many individuals who remember him with affection and gratitude. Some of Mac's many acts of charity and kindness throughout his life, as well as examples of his unswerving toughness, came to light after his death. Mac, in his own quiet way, was a big supporter of civil rights. He knew the leaders of the black community in Waterbury well. After he died, a black woman who ran a local community center stood up at a memorial service for Mac. She said that a few years earlier, she was at her wits' end, trying to scrape together the money needed to repair an old furnace that kept the center warm during New England's cold winters. She called Mac to see if he could help. He asked her how much it would cost to replace the furnace. She told him it would cost $10,000 (about $60,000 in 2014 dollars) and more than the community center could afford or raise. He told her he would give her the $10,000 as a gift to install a new furnace on one condition: that she not tell anyone who the donor was. She kept her promise until after he died.

Examples continue to surface, even now, more than twenty-five years after his death. In 2014, a college teammate of Molly's referred to the fact that Mac had paid her college tuition. Assuming that Molly knew all about this, she was reiterating her gratitude, saying that she could never have gone to college without his help. It was a complete surprise to Molly—she had played sports with this woman and never knew. Another friend, from a difficult home, has told Molly more than once how special she felt around Mac. He paid attention to her, asked about her life, and told her to stand up straight and be proud of her height—something that Megan and Molly had heard a million times but which her own parents never bothered to do.

In 1968, when Mac was running Scovill, the civil rights leader Martin Luther King Jr. was assassinated by a gunman at a motel in Memphis, Tennessee. King's murder was a devastating loss to the black community. Although the black preacher was only thirty-nine years old, he was a pivotal figure in the civil rights movement in the United States and an important advocate of peaceful protest. Mac arranged for the leaders of the black community in Waterbury, Connecticut, to be flown to King's funeral in Atlanta. Mac accompanied them, and it was done quietly, without publicity. For Mac, being at Dr. King's funeral was a glimpse into another world, and he had the chance to clearly experience what it felt like to be in the minority. After Mac's death, Hubie Williamson, a black leader in Waterbury, remembered the rare chance to talk with Mac for an uninterrupted hour or so, walking around the airport, waiting for the return trip. He says that they discussed humanity, dignity, and race—issues not normally broached in their regular brief dealings. Those community leaders never forgot the gesture. When Mac was named Commerce Secretary, his friends in the black community hosted a sendoff party featuring a huge sheet cake at the Black Elks Club in Waterbury.

The Minority Business Development Agency (MBDA), a small Commerce Department agency, provides federal support to minority businesses for the promotion of job creation. The Hasidic community, based in the Williamsburg neighborhood of New York City, had sought unsuccessfully for years to be designated a "minority" group to make them eligible for federal funds. The Hasidic community is an orthodox branch of Judaism with a very conservative lifestyle, and like many conservative religious sects, it avoids engagement with the outside world. Rabbi Zvi Kestenbaum, a short man with the characteristic long beard, curled sidelocks, traditional wide-brimmed black hat, and long black robe, was the primary liaison with the government for the Hasidic community. Rabbi Kestenbaum had lobbied various agencies in Washington, unsuccessfully, to get minority status for his community. As part of this effort, he invited Mac to visit the community at Williamsburg. Whenever the group hosted a government official, regardless of importance, they stretched a huge welcome banner across the main street. When Mac arrived, he was greeted with an enormous "Welcome Secretary of Commerce Malcolm Baldrige" banner. On the walking tour, about twenty long-robed, bearded men hovered around him at every step, within inches, as is their custom. He met with the Grand Rabbi, the top official in the community, was briefed on the kinds of programs the group offered to its people, and which ones needed more funding. Mac was shown the various group facilities, health care areas, and the schools with young children in their classes.

The Hassidic community's young people were very intelligent and well ahead of their peers in the outside world. Mac was impressed by the intellect of the children but was chagrined when he learned that no Hasidic children attended college because they were expected to remain in their community. Leaving the community for any reason was discouraged. After his first visit, Mac told an aide traveling with him, "I'm going to make sure these kids go to college. They are being held back by not being allowed to leave, and they and society lose." Mac had no qualms of taking on traditions that dated back centuries to achieve that goal. The visit convinced him that the Hasidic Jews should be designated a minority group, and Commerce became the first federal agency to grant the designation to the Hasidim, opening a door for others to follow suit and providing resources to the community that would improve opportunities for those bright youngsters he wanted to help.

There are many similar examples of thoughtfulness. Marlin Fitzwater, the press secretary to both presidents Reagan and George H. W. Bush, has a vivid recollection from February 1987, shortly after his appointment to the position. Congressional hearings on the Iran-Contra scandal had begun, and the White House press corps decided to grill the new press secretary to see if he might crack under pressure. Fitzwater returned to his West Wing office completely drained, wondering if his new job could possibly get worse. Suddenly, his office door opened and Mac walked in, wearing a business suit with cowboy boots and his big championship belt buckle showing a team roper catching a steer. "Marlin," he said, "I'm Mac Baldrige. I just want to tell you, be cool. Just be cool and you'll be fine." Then he turned and walked out. Fitzwater not only appreciated the support at a low moment, but he said many times that in subsequent briefings, he clenched his teeth and thought of Mac saying, "Just be cool."

Bill Archey, the Acting Assistant Secretary for Trade Administration, held the position of Acting Customs Commissioner when Reagan took office. He is one of many career government employees whom Mac appointed to top jobs, positions that typically would be reserved for political appointees. Bill had a younger brother named Jack, who had Down syndrome. Mac befriended Jack, a sweet and loving man, and went out of his way to invite Jack to visit the Commerce Department and to include him in a horseback riding program for mentally disabled children that Midge supported.

Wesley Goad, Mac's driver, discovered that a young security guard, Hezekiah Baxter, known to all as "Chick," was an excellent amateur artist. Goad suggested Chick draw a picture of Mac. He did, and it was so good that Mac hung it on his office wall and helped Chick get the tuition money he needed to attend the Corcoran School of Art at night.

Former senator Alan Simpson, a Republican from Wyoming, became a great friend of Mac after spending weekends with the Baldriges at the vice president's summer house in Kennebunkport, Maine. Senator Simpson recalled a time in 1987 when Mac went out of his way to be kind to Robert "Bud" McFarlane, at one of the lowest points in McFarlane's life. McFarlane, a Naval Academy graduate and career marine, served as the National Security Advisor to Reagan, the pinnacle of a long and highly successful career in Washington. After the Iran-Contra affair came to light, he was forced to resign his job, because the scheme had been hatched by one of his assistants on McFarlane's watch. Despondent, he attempted suicide with an overdose of Valium in February 1987. He did not succeed, and the botched suicide seemed emblematic of a stellar career gone bad and a man who had truly hit bottom.

Simpson remembered being at a Washington party with Mac when they spotted McFarlane. Washington can be a cruel and cold city. When someone is out, he is really out. The most social and political players would ignore or avoid a disgraced NSC advisor. (McFarlane was sentenced to a suspended prison term and fine the following year and was eventually pardoned by the first President Bush.) According to Simpson, Mac went directly over to McFarlane as soon as he saw him and told him that nothing was so bad that it was worth ending his life. He told him that he was a terrific guy, and people loved him, and he needed to learn to love and be loved. It was an extraordinarily intimate thing to say to another government official in a social setting, and it was clearly heartfelt and sincere. "Mac was at the top of his game then and McFarlane listened intently," said Simpson.

His toughness was legendary, and after he died, many stories were told about the steely side of this quiet man. Molly Baldrige, his daughter, recalled the time when raiders were trying to take control of Scovill. The group intended to get majority control by acquiring more than 50 percent of the stock and then sell off each division for the highest price, thus destroying the company. At the last minute, Mac managed to keep the raiders from acquiring the necessary stock. When the head of the raider group learned this, he called Mac at 2 a.m. to bemoan the fact that Mac had ruined his life. He said he was going to put a gun to his head if he could not get the shares needed to give him control. Mac said, "Wait, don't do that. Wait until I can get there . . ." At this point, the raider thought Mac was giving in. Mac continued, ". . . and help you pull the trigger."

Many of the stories people tell of Mac today have to do with his integrity. He was never cowed or buffaloed, even by the high and mighty. While Mac was on a first-name basis with many top-flight industrialists and was an unabashed advocate of American business interests, he knew where and when to draw the line. He expected business leaders to adhere to a code of behavior and to take responsibility for their own affairs and leave his business to him. Lionel Olmer remembered a private dinner with Lee Iacocca, the head of Chrysler, early in the first term when the Reagan administration was dealing with the issue of Japanese auto imports. Iacocca wanted to have dinner with the Secretary, so a small group—Iacocca, Mac, Olmer, and Bill Timmons, a legendary lobbyist for the auto industry—gathered for dinner at the Georgetown Club, a private club in Washington. Within minutes, the two principals were addressing one another as "Lee" and "Mac." Their rapport was instantaneous. After dinner, Iacocca lit up a big cigar, and Mac mentioned that the Commerce Department was reorganizing the International Trade Administration by sector, with deputy assistant secretaries in charge of each sector. Mac struggled to remember the name of the young Treasury Department official who had been hired to head up the auto industry sector. He turned to Olmer and said, "What is that guy's name? Mike . . . Mike . . . ?" Olmer was about to say, "Driggs" when Iacocca sat bolt upright, pulled the cigar out of his mouth and roared, "Not Driggs!? That son of a bitch took my plane away from me!" (In 1979, Congress reluctantly approved $1.5 billion in loan guarantees for the Chrysler Corporation to keep the auto manufacturer from going bankrupt. In return for being bailed out by taxpayers, Congress demanded that the company give up certain perquisites, including the chief executive's private jet. Driggs was the person at the Treasury Department responsible for running the Chrysler loan guarantee program.) Without missing a beat, Mac said, "No wonder we hired him."

Years after Mac's death, Alan Simpson remembered him as a thoughtful man of action. "He wasn't going to sit and philosophize and go through the meaning of life and waste time going through that crap," said Simpson. "He just grabbed life by the nape of the neck and did it. He was a no bullshit guy with a sense of immediacy. . . . He had wisdom. A lot of people have knowledge but damn few have wisdom. He did."

When Post University in Waterbury, Connecticut, named its business school after Mac, Molly suggested that if Mac were to teach a business course, he would emphasize four things:

- Keep it short and sweet.
- Be brave, and if you've done your homework, don't second-guess yourself.
- Underpromise and overdeliver.
- Focus on the few things that you really love and do them as best you can.

An Associated Press reporter once asked Mac to define success. Some businessmen might say it was making millions of dollars or inventing a new product. Mac had a different definition. He said, "Success is finding something you really like to do and caring enough about it to do it well, sticking your neck out if you're sure you're right and getting lucky."

Mac certainly considered himself a lucky man, but he made his own luck. After he died, a *Washington Post* editorial read, "Malcolm Baldrige was one of those rare public people who have and retain a set of strong private values and interests while they are at the top of government, a man who had an individual identity that could not be swayed or otherwise affected by the glories of office . . . what we are saying is that he was a very special guy, a force for pragmatism in an administration in which the prevailing economic ideas were highly ideological." A *New York Times* editorial, titled "The Decency of Malcolm Baldrige," said that he "brought decency and a cool head to the upper reaches of politics. In an administration marred by zealotry, he stood for soft-spoken reason . . . Mac Baldrige was a credit to the business community and to public service."

In the spring of 1984, an election year when Mac spent time on the stump for Reagan and fielded many questions about politics and image, he told the *Hartford Courant*: "Cowboys don't use the word 'image.' It's a reputation. You can create an image. You've got to earn a reputation."

Death denied Mac the time to finish his work and to reach the goal of becoming the longest serving Commerce Secretary in history. It robbed him of his retirement dream of hitting the rodeo circuit across the country with Midge in a Winnebago, of the quiet joy of growing old with Midge, of meeting all his grandchildren and seeing them grow up. But during his lifetime, Mac thoroughly earned his reputation as a man of quiet strength, impeccable integrity, solid judgment, and practical action, an honorable and decent man in the best American cowboy tradition.

ACKNOWLEDGMENTS

WE RELIED UPON MANY NEWSPAPER AND MAGAZINE articles written during the six years and seven months of Mac Baldrige's time as Commerce Secretary in writing this book. But we also drew upon the memories and experiences of a number of people who worked in Washington during those years. While some had died, there were a significant number of contemporaries of Mac's who regaled us with their recollections.

We would like to thank them for taking the time to look back, dig through their own files, and talk to us about Mac Baldrige and his tenure at Commerce. Some, such as Lionel Olmer, kindly responded to repeated follow-up questions via email and telephone to check out a theory or fact.

In no particular order, they are: Art Pine, Arlene Triplett, Senator Alan Simpson, Bruce Smart, former Deputy Commerce Secretary Bud Brown, Charles Ludolph, Christian

Holmes, David Bates, David Markey, Gerald McKiernan, Harry Hertz, J. D. Young, Jim Moore, Joe Wright, Lionel Olmer, Mary Ann Fish, Matthew Heyman, Mike Smith, Mitchell Stanley, Olin Wethington, Otto Wolf, Patricia Corken, Paul O'Day, Robert Dederick, Robert Ortner, Ruth Robbins, Tom Collamore, William Archey, Leonard Leganza, Kay Bulow, Jean Becker, Sen. Don Riegle, Rep. Don Bonker, Gerald Mossinghoff, and Eugene Lawson.

We strove for accuracy. Any mistakes are ours, and we apologize in advance for them.

This book never would have been written had it not been for Megan and Molly Baldrige, Mac's daughters. They wanted an accurate representation of their father's Washington years for their children. They shared their mother's remarkable scrapbooks and personal correspondence. They also read every word and, being their father's daughters, helped enormously to make certain the manuscript met their father's high standards for clear and comprehensible English.

AUTHORS' NOTE

THIS BOOK WAS COMMISSIONED BY THE BALDRIGE FAMILY, so anyone looking for a harsh critique of Malcolm Baldrige or the Reagan administration will not find it here, but then again you won't find a lot of negative comment about Mac Baldrige anywhere, based on our research. In fact, Mac's daughters asked us to include his failures as well as his successes because they wanted a realistic and balanced portrait of their father's time in Washington, not a fairy tale. When Mac died in 1987, he was survived by two grandchildren, both very young. His other grandchildren were born after his death. While all grew up hearing stories about their grandfather, none of them have any clear memory of him. This book was written with them in mind to tell them about his years as the Commerce Secretary in Ronald Reagan's cabinet.

Mac was a straightforward and honest man, and to honor his memory and tell his story properly, we strove to be as accurate as possible and to stay true to his plain English rules, as he would have liked. Our personal experiences informed the compilation of Mac's story. B. Jay Cooper first met Mac while working as a reporter in Waterbury, Connecticut, where Mac's company, Scovill, Inc., was based. When Mac went to Washington, he brought B. Jay along as his speechwriter. B. Jay became director of public affairs at the Commerce Department and later worked as a deputy press secretary for presidents Reagan and George H. W. Bush. He has firsthand knowledge of many of the events in this book. Chris Black spent thirty years working as a political reporter in Boston and Washington for the *Boston Globe* and as a White House and congressional correspondent for CNN. She covered both Reagan and Bush when they were presidential candidates.

To provide sufficient context for young people to appreciate the times and conditions in which Mac lived, B. Jay tracked down many of the officials who served with Mac in government for interviews, as well as a reporter who covered his time at Commerce. They were generous with their insights and recollections and shared many stories, many B. Jay had never heard, about the Secretary. Midge Baldrige, Mac's wife, maintained careful scrapbooks of their years in Washington that contain a chronological and contemporary news account of his work on trade and his advocacy for business. As two former news reporters, we believe there are few other sources that could have been as helpful in re-creating a moment in American history. In those years, many news organizations fielded large Washington bureaus, and the reporters who specialized in trade, economics, business, and finance acquired deep knowledge, excellent sources, and penetrating understanding of the political calculations being made at the time. Many will interpret those years differently, but this book is about a particular man at a particular time so we tried to reflect his reality and point of view as much as possible.

In 1980 when Ronald Reagan won election as president, the term *globalization* was not yet in common use, but the effects on U.S. business and manufacturing of a smaller, more interconnected world were undeniable. Japan had suddenly emerged as a threat to the economic supremacy America had enjoyed without challenge since World War II. The computer and high-tech industries were beginning to fuel a communications revolution with sweeping ramifications for culture and business. Cable television news was only beginning with CNN, and the Internet was not in use at all. Developing countries were embracing manufacturing to build their own industrial bases and to find prosperity, drawing jobs away from the United States. As the Reagan administration dealt with the rapidly changing international economy, Mac Baldrige, a quiet, effective, and influential man, played a central role.

Mac was an American original—a cowboy, an industrialist, a husband, father, grandfather, friend, and boss. Few like him have passed through the halls of power in Washington. We suspect none like him ever will again.

APPENDIX I
Secretary's Writing Style

CLARITY AND BREVITY ARE KEY FACTORS WHEN PREPARING correspondence for the Secretary or Deputy Secretary. The Secretary wants short sentences and short words, with emphasis on *plain English*. Use no more words than effective expression requires.

- Answer questions specifically.
- The response should be no more than one page, where possible.

When answering a series of questions, prepare a brief cover letter and attach question-and-answer page (or pages).

- If the response is negative, be polite, not abrupt.
- Avoid wordiness. Keep sentences lean and short.
- Use the active rather than the passive voice.

- Use no unnecessary adjectives or adverbs. Write with nouns and verbs to strengthen letter.
- Do not use nouns or adjectives as verbs, such as:

  to impact
  to interface
  it obsoletes

- Use the precise word or phrase.

  datum (singular); data (plural)
  criterion (singular); criteria (plural)
  subsequent means *after*, not *before*
  different *from*, not different *than*
  insure means to guarantee against financial loss
  ensure means to make sure or certain (Although *insure* and
    ensure share the same meaning, this usage is preferred.)
  affect means to influence; to act upon; to alter; to assume;
    to adopt
  think is mental; *feel* is physical or emotional (think
    thoughts; feel feelings)

- Please stop using affected or imprecise words. Some examples:

  alternatives (use *choices*)
  delighted (use *pleased* or *happy*)
  dialogue
  effectuated
  enhance
  facilitate
  glad (use *pleased* or *happy*)
  hereinafter
  hopefully (use *I hope*)
  image
  input (limit, unless used as a computer term)

ongoing (prefer *continuing*)

orient

output

overview

parameter (use *boundary* or *limit*; unless used as a computer term)

specificity

target or targeted

thrust

unique

viable

- Please stop using ALL *-ize* words. Some examples:

  finalize   prioritize

  maximize   utilize (prefer *use*)

  minimize   utilization

  optimize

- Please stop using the following phrases:

  as you know, as I am sure you know, as you are aware

  at the present time, at this time (use *now*)

  bottom line

  contingent upon

  I am deeply concerned

  I appreciate your concern (or interest or views)

  I believe, we believe (unless speculating on future action)

  I regret I cannot be more responsive or encouraging

  I share your concern (or interest or views)

  I understand (unless speculating on future action)

  I would hope (use *I hope*)

  in essence, the essence

  in terms of

  in the near future (use *soon*)

  in view of (use *because*)

  it is my intention

more importantly (use *more important*)
mutually beneficial
needless to say
point in time
positive feedback
prior to (use *before*)
subject matter
Thank you for your letter expressing concern (use *Thank you for your letter regarding . . .*)
time frame
subject matter

- Avoid:

    closing the letter too abruptly (Thank the writer for his or her interest or support.)
    one-sentence paragraphs in body of letter
    overquoting writer's letter

- Eliminate gender-specific language whenever possible.

    worker (instead of workman)
    chairperson (instead of chairman)
    reporter or newscaster (instead of newsman)
    police officer (instead of policeman)
    astronaut (instead of spaceman)
    mail carrier (instead of postman)
    committeeperson (instead of committeeman)

- Avoid redundancies, such as:

    | enclosed herewith | new initiatives |
    | end result | personally reviewed |
    | future plans | serious crisis |
    | important essentials | |

- Avoid split infinitives (placing an adverb between *to* and the verb), *unless a split infinitive makes the sentence less awkward.*

- Do not use addressee's first name in the body of the letter.
- Do not refer to the date of the incoming letter.
- Stop apologizing, such as:

  I regret the delay in responding to you.

- Do not close a letter with the following phrases:

  Please let me know if I can be of further assistance.
  I hope this information is helpful.

- Annual Reports to Congress (transmittal letter)

  Use: I am pleased to submit

- Closing the letter

  Do not use: With best wishes

The following quote from *The Elements of Style* by Strunk and White reflects the Secretary's style:

Vigorous writing is concise. A sentence should contain no unnecessary words, a paragraph no unnecessary sentences, for the same reason that a drawing should have no unnecessary lines and a machine no unnecessary parts. This requires not that the writer make all his sentences short, or that he avoid all detail and treat his subject only in outlines, but that every word tell.

Secretary Baldrige says, "In short, halfway between Ernest Hemingway and Zane Grey with *no bureaucratese.*"

APPENDIX II

President Reagan's Eulogy for Secretary of Commerce Malcolm Baldrige, July 29, 1987, Washington's National Cathedral

MIDGE, MEGAN, MOLLY, DISTINGUISHED LADIES AND gentlemen. The day I called Mac Baldrige to ask him to join the cabinet, I was told by Midge that I would have to call back later. He was out on his horse roping and couldn't come to the phone. Right then I knew he was the kind of man I wanted.

It's a gift to be simple, we're told. If that means to hold simple, strong and decent values, Mac had that gift. You could see it in the way he moved around the White House. He seemed to know everyone—not just those in the public eye, but the secretaries and assistants as well. And he treated everyone with the same measure of courtesy and respect— from his driver to the President. He never judged a man or woman by rank or trappings. Despite his many remarkable successes, worldly success was not the way he measured peo- ple. No, money was not, position not, qualities of character were. Honesty, courage, industry and humility, those were his yardsticks. And if you had these simple qualities, you'd make it in his eyes—whether you were rich or poor, famous or unknown.

Language was one way he decided if you were his kind of person. It's well known now that he insisted on simple language in memos at the Commerce Department. He banned phrases that were vague or redundant. He once said that the thing he liked about cowboys was that they didn't talk unless they had something to say, and when they said it, they meant it.

To him, simple language did not mark a simple mind, but a strong and fearless one. It was a sign of those who didn't hide their meaning behind a cloud of ambiguous words.

Mac, of course, never hid his opinions. Even if the tide was against him, he was forceful and clear and unflinching. I always knew where he stood, and so did the country. I could always count on him for the truth as he saw it—no matter how unpleasant or unpopular. There were times when the Cabinet came down on an issue 12-to-1, and he was on the short end. But I knew that if he believed something the others didn't, he wouldn't rein himself in and follow the herd. He would step forward and be clear.

What I'm saying about Mac Baldrige adds up to a simple but extraordinary quality that I would call, more than anything else, "American." In his directness, in his honesty, in his independence, in his disregard for rank, in his courage, he embodied the best of the American spirit. I suppose we think of that spirit as living most of all in cowboys. And that's why I've always suspected that it was more than just roping and his place here in Washington that got Mac voted into the Cowboy Hall of Fame. He belonged there. It was in his blood. It was in his heart and soul.

Let me say a word about his many contributions to his country. These were not simple, although they were built on simple principles—principles like his reverence for the independence of the American character, for the freedom that lets independence flourish, and for the opportunities of a free society.

Mac was an architect of American international economic policy during years in which that policy moved to center stage. He also helped shape our policy towards east-west trade in a period in which that was a source of new questions and concerns. And perhaps the least recognized of his major accomplishments was the securing of trade ties with China. In just four years since his 1983 visit to China, trade has become a pillar of the Sino-American relationship.

To contribute so much required skill and persistence—qualities Mac had in abundance. It also required vision—vision not only for dealing with immediate issues, but for the future of the entire world and its economy, as well.

I always prized the quality of Mac's vision. He had the capacity to look up from the dust of the plains to the distant mountains. He never forgot that all the skirmishes and battles over trade policy that we have here in Washington and around the world have one final goal. We're building a world in which our children and grandchildren will live. And we who love freedom and revere the dignity of humanity have a sacred duty to make that an open world of real hope and abundant opportunity, a world in which the spirit of freedom—yes, what you might call that part of the American spirit that lives in all of mankind—in which that spirit can ride across an open range towards the peaks beyond.

I'm told that Mac's staff had orders to interrupt him at whatever the time of day with calls from only two people. I was one. And any cowboy who rang up was the other. Well, I'm honored to have been in that company. Mac, as we know, left us while he was doing what he loved most. And now, when any of us wants to ring him up, we'll have to remind ourselves that he's out on a horse somewhere and we'll just have to wait. Yet in his simplicity, he has entered the company of the men and women who have shaped our nation and its destiny. And he will live in that company forever.

Yes, there is sorrow, but the sorrow is with us and for us. We must believe that door is opened that God promised and he has just gone through that door into another life where there is no more pain, no more sorrow, and we must believe that we, too, will one day go through that door and join him again.

Thank you. God bless you.

APPENDIX III
Letters of Condolence to Mac's Family

UNITED STATES DEPARTMENT OF COMMERCE
The Under Secretary
National Oceanic and Atmospheric Administration
Washington, D.C. 20230

July 30, 1987

To the Grandchildren of Malcolm Baldrige:

You're so young -- perhaps as yet unborn. I worked for your
Grandfather, and want to tell you how I feel about him. He was
the best boss I have ever had, and I've had some great ones.

I've been a member of his senior management team. My job is
managing the National Oceanic and Atmospheric Administration
(NOAA). He was fascinated by NOAA's activities which include
protecting marine mammals and fish, making charts for pilots
and mariners, forecasting weather, and understanding data from
satellites. While he was Secretary of Commerce, how we launch
and operate satellites was changing, and he had a big part in
the new way we deal with outer space. Think about that when
you look up in the sky.

Sometimes he would call my office to ask for a weather report
for the next day in Middleburg or some other place he'd go riding or calf-roping. Our predictions were usually pretty good.
When you are teenagers, NOAA forecasts will be better. Your
Grandfather knew that, because he learned about high technology
equipment so we could prepare for the future -- your future.

One part of my job is Commissioner of Whaling. Your Grandfather
cared so much about saving the whales that he encouraged us to
take a clear stand with other countries and within our own
Government. I am proud to continue that effort.

He was not only an important man. He was important to many
people who depended on his strong character and quiet determination. It was exciting working for him, but it wasn't easy.
What made it difficult was that he trusted us even if we didn't
trust ourselves to do what he expected. That is why the men
and women of NOAA wanted to name a ship after him. When it is
convenient for your Grandmother, we will christen the MALCOLM
BALDRIGE. It is a Class I vessel that visits many places in the
world. It is the ship we were aboard for the Centennial of the
Statue of Liberty on July 4, 1986, in New York Harbor. What a
wonderful celebration. You can watch the video tape someday.

I hope you ask a lot of questions about your Grandfather. He
deserves knowing. You may not hear his voice again, but you
can find out what he said. Those who knew him will miss him
very much, but we are ready to share our memories with you.

Sincerely,

Anthony J. Calio

THE ADMINISTRATOR

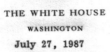

THE WHITE HOUSE

WASHINGTON

July 27, 1987

Dear Midge:

Nancy and I, and all of Mac's many friends throughout the
Administration, are devastated by his death. We join you in
your grief and offer our heartfelt condolences to you and your
family.

I think you know pretty well by now that Mac was my idea of
a perfect public servant. He didn't think of government as
a way of life or as a place to experiment with the lives of
others. He worked his way up from mill hand to head of an
international business with operations in 23 countries, and it
was only after he accumulated all of that experience that he
came to Washington as a member of my Cabinet team. Mac knew
what it took to make the Department of Commerce work because
he knew what made companies tick, and because he understood
our economic system not as some dry theory in motion but as a
series of tough day-to-day decisions by managers working to
get out products and meet payrolls.

I deeply valued his realism, his passion for facts, his
wide-ranging insight into the world economy, and -- above
all -- his love for this nation and its people. He played a key
role at my side these past six and one-half years, and despite
his characteristic willingness to let others get the credit, I am
convinced that the American people join me in recognizing how
much our economic renaissance owes to his efforts as Secretary.
He didn't just do his job, he remade and renewed it, and his
tenure has set the highest standard for all who follow.

Mac was my friend, and I'll be forever proud to say I was one
of his. America has suffered a great loss. May God grant
you, Megan and Mary, and the entire Baldrige family true peace
and consolation. Our hearts go out to you and our prayers are
with you now and in the days ahead.

Sincerely,

Ron

Mrs. Malcolm Baldrige
2101 Connecticut Avenue, N.W.
Washington, D.C. 20008

so Dakota to Iowa
Friday July 31 '87

Dear Midge
    You'll never know how truly
honored I was when you asked
me to say a few words at Mac's
funeral. This government is great
and meaningful, too; but as I

think about life it's family
and friendship that matters
    Here are my remarks
Excuse the tear stains; but
I really did love the guy.
    Be strong. Where can we
fit in? Love George

SCOTTISH POET ROBERT BURNS WROTE ... "PRINCES AND LORDS ARE

BUT THE BREATH OF KINGS ... AND HONEST MAN IS THE NOBLEST

WORK OF GOD.... MAC WAS AN HONEST MAN.

HE NEVER QUITE ~~FIT~~ ANY MOLD ..... You'd HAVE THOUGHT THIS SON

OF ~~HOTCHKISS AND YALE~~ *EASTERN SCHOOLS* WOULD FIT INTO AN EASTERN MOLD. NOT

SO..... WITH HIS BUSINESS SUIT HE WORE THAT HAND TOOLED

(EVEN THEY COULDN'T KEEP THOSE DROOPY PANTS UP PROPERLY)

BELT AND MASSIVE BUCKLE, HE RODE HORSES AND HE LOVED HIS

PLACE IN NEW MEXICO. HE FELT AT HOME WITH THE COWBOYS HE

NEVER FORGET I'M ON THE TENNIS

ROPED WITH ALLHIS LIFE.... THE BROTHERS OF THOSE WHO SALUTED

HIM SATURDAY NIGHT AT CONTRA COSTA COUNTY, CALIFORNIA.

(over those sher high of his)

Ladies ... today auto...

_@_ -2-

The RIDERLESS ~~BALCK~~ *BLACK* HORSE MADE ITS WAY AROUND THE ARENA

AND GROWN MEN WEPT..... YOU:D "VE THOUGHT THE PRESIDENT

BUSY - SUCCESSFUL

OF SCOVIL MIGHT HAVE BEEN TOO BUSY AND TOO SUCCESSFUL TO

GIVE TIME TO COMMUNITY AND COUNTRY. NOT SO. *HE WAS IN IT*

AROUND HERE RIGHT UP TO HIS EYEBALLS - HELPING OTHERS

ONE TIME MAC TOOK ME BY THE WOODBURY VOLUNTEER FIRE DEPT.

WHERE MIDGE WAS AN ACTIVE MEMBER. THERE WASN""T A FIREMAN

IN THE PLACE WHO MIDGE AND MAC DIDNT LOVE AND VICE VERSA.

.....ANOTHER TIME WHEN WE WERE WORKING THE POLITICAL TRENCHES

IN SOME SMALL TOWN, ONE OF ITALY'S SONS ,NOW A DEDICATED

PRECINCT WORKER IN THE U.S. OF A TOLD ME ... "THAT MAC

-3-

IS ONE CLASS SON OF A _____" (YOU KNOW WHAT HE SAID)...THEN

HE ADDED ROSE AND I LOVE THE GUY."

MAC STAYED FIT. BUT HE DID IT HIS WAY. YES HE RODE, BUT

DID YOU EVER SEE HIM JOG? IT WAS LIKE WATCHING GRASS GROW

BUT HE FINISHED STRONG... ALL THROUGH HIS LIFE HE FINISHED

STRONG....... NO THERE IS NO SINGLE REASON WHY MACS SHOULDERS

WERE TOO BROAD TO FIT ANY PARTICULAR MOLD. IT WAS HIS ZEST

FOR LIFE, HIS LOVE OF FAMILY AND OF ALL PEOPLE,HIS SERVICE

TO HIS COUNTRY IN COMBAT, HIS PRINCIPLED LEADERSHIP AS SEC.

OF COMMERCE FOR 6½ DEDICATED YEARS.IT WAS HONOR AND INTEGRITY

-4-

Macs word OF HONORE WAS AS GOOD AS A $20 GOLD PIECE .....
                A
AND HE WAS STRONG GUY, BUT HE DINT HAVE TO RAISE HIS VOICE

TO PROJECT HIS STRENGTH......ON MEMORIAL DAY LAST YEAR HE
                                                       COAST
SPOKE AT OUR LITTLE CHURCH NEAR MAINES ROCKBOUND CHURCH.
                    1st Hand
HE TOLD A MOVING STORY OF CONFLICTS OF WAR... THE AGONY
              ^
OF TAKING A LIFE, THE POSSIBILITY OF RECONCILIATION AND

FORGIVENESS. AS ALWAYS MAC DIDNT USE MANY WORDS .... BUT

HE SAID SO MUCH........ HIS DAUGTHERS REVERD HIM...

MIDGE ADORED HIM ... AND I LOVED HIM LIKE A BROTHER....

THIS HONEST MAN WAS INDEED THE NOBLEST WORK OF GOD.

Supreme Court of the United States
Washington, D. C. 20543

CHAMBERS OF
JUSTICE SANDRA DAY O'CONNOR

July 27, 1987

Dear Midge,

Reading the tragic news
of your husband's accident
brought sorrow into the lives
of millions throughout the
land. Mac brought such
a steady hand and good
sense to our nation's
economic decisions. It
is never easy to serve
the nation in such a visible
and challenging post. He
did it with enormous
success — and always

with a smile and sense
of humour. It was always
a special occasion to
chat with him.

John and I join all
your friends in expressing
our great sense of loss
and our sympathy to
you and your family.
He left life perhaps as
he would have wished —
on the back of a horse;
He left his brand on
the nation and all of us.

　　　　　　Sincerely,

　　　　　　Sandra

MARTIN LUTHER KING JR CENTER G S
449 AUBURN AVE NORTHEAST
ATLANTA GA 30312 28AM

4-01496A8209 07/28/87 ICS IPMMTZZ CSP WHSB
4045241956 MGMS TDMT ATLANTA GA 134 07-28 1216P EST

MRS MARGARET BALDRIDGE
2101 CONNECTICUT AVE NORTHWEST
WASHINGTON DC 20008

I WAS DEEPLY SADDENED TO LEARN OF THE DEATH OF YOUR BELOVED HUSBAND,
MALCOLM BALDRIDGE. I OFFER MY MOST HEARTFELT CONDOLENCES TO YOU, YOUR
FAMILY AND YOUR HUSBAND'S MANY FRIENDS AND SUPPORTERS.

SECRETARY BALDRIDGE WAS ONE OF THE NATION'S MOST SELFLESS AND
DEDICATED PUBLIC SERVANTS. WITH HIS PASSING AMERICA HAS LOST ONE OF
OUR MOST CREATIVE AND INNOVATIVE LEADERS WHOSE TIRELESS COMMITMENT TO
FAIRNESS AND EFFICIENCY IN GOVERNMENT WAS A MAJOR FORCE FOR SOCIAL
AND ECONOMIC PROGRESS. MALCOLM BALDRIDGE WILL BE SORELY MISSED BUT
HIS LEGACY WILL REMAIN AN ENDURING MODEL OF COMMITMENT FOR FUTURE
GENERATIONS TO EMULATE. I PRAY THAT YOU AND YOUR FAMILY WILL FIND THE
COMFORT IN THE KNOWLEDGE THAT HIS SPIRIT AND HIS COURAGEOUS EXAMPLES
ARE ETERNAL
    CORETTA SCOTT KING

12:14 EST

MGMCOMP

United States Senate
WASHINGTON, DC 20510

July 28, 1987

Mrs. Malcolm Baldridge
2101 Connecticut Avenue N.W.
Washington, D.C. 20008

Dear Mrs. Baldridge:

I write to express my heartfelt
sympathy on the tragic accident which
has taken your beloved husband.

Believe me, I know it is particularly
difficult to lose loved ones so suddenly,
and I can share with you your deep shock and
sorrow.

From my own experiences, I can tell you
that you will think of your husband often,
but as time goes on, you will remember more
the life and loved you shared, rather than
the sad time at the end.

Secretary Baldridge will be judged by
history as a man who served our nation with
distinction and honor, and as a man whose
extraordinary record of public service
transcended party lines.

You have my deepest condolences.

Sincerely,

Ted Kennedy

815 16th St., N.W.

LANE KIRKLAND
AMERICAN FEDERATION OF LABOR AND
CONGRESS OF INDUSTRIAL ORGANIZATIONS
WASHINGTON, D. C. 20006

July 27, 1987

Dear Midge:

Irena and I were shocked and saddened to learn of Mac's untimely death.

As I am sure you know, he had our personal affection as well as our deep respect for his candor and determination to fight for his convictions.

Those of us in the labor movement may not have always agreed with Mac, but we always knew where he stood and we could always argue our case and get a thoughtful and considerate response.

Mac was tough and he was fair. He was an outstanding Secretary of Commerce. He understood the importance of fair trade and he fought to provide our country with an intelligent trade policy.

You and your family have our sympathy and heartfelt condolences.

Sincerely,

Lane Kirkland

Mrs. Malcolm Baldrige
2101 Connecticut Avenue, N.W.
Washington, D. C. 20008

The Washington Post

1150 15TH STREET, N. W.

WASHINGTON, D. C. 20071

(202) 334-6000

WRITER'S DIRECT TELEPHONE NUMBER

_____

August 2, 1987

Mrs. Malcolm Baldrige
Department of Commerce
Washington, D. C.

Dear Mrs. Baldrige:

Please accept my wife Carol's and my condolences on the tragic death of your husband.

In 30 years as a reporter I met few people in public life who were as straight, honest, warm and thoughtful as Secretary Baldrige. As I came to know him, I felt I was one of the luckiest reporters on The Post to have a cabinet secretary such as him to cover. He represented a fundamental integrity that too often is missing in Washington.

We all are losers in his death, and we wish you the best because your loss is greatest.

Sincerely,

Stuart Auerbach

DEPARTMENT OF STATE

DIRECTOR GENERAL OF THE FOREIGN SERVICE
AND DIRECTOR OF PERSONNEL
WASHINGTON

July 29

Dear Midge,

This Town and nation lost one of the finest in Mac. He was an original, unique in so many ways. Among other things, he was the ablest natural diplomat in my experience. It was a rare and rewarding experience to work with him, negotiating with the Europeans, to witness his special blend of wry humor, integrity and unfailing thoughtfulness. There are so many of us in The Foreign Service who admired and will miss him. His like don't come to Washington under any Administration. And if he was admired, he and you were too as a special pair. This brings, inadequately, my deepest admiration for a life so well-lived and for your loss my deepest sympathy.

Sincerely,

George Vest

August 12, 1987

Dear Mrs. Baldrige

   In this letter I want to express my deepist sympathy to
you and your family in your time of sorrow. Mac will always
be remembered by many people, including myself.
   Many people will remember him for the great things he
has contributed to this country, but I will remember the
little things he did for me. When I first met Mac we were
roping at Nancy Staples barn and then I continued roping
with him at Charlies and Kens. My horse developed a foot
problem and I was unable to use him for three years. During
that time Mac told me I could use his horse, gave me helpful
advice and gave me one of his heeling ropes. One night Ken
decided to have a little jack-pot. I did not have enough
money on me to pay the entry fee, Mac offered to pay the two
dollars for me. On July 23, 1987, I was in Washington for a
leadership conference for youth leaders of the Future
Farmers of America. I went to see Mac and he showed me his
office, pictures, and the roping he did when he got
frustrated. He gave me advice and told me things that I will
remember for the rest of my life. Next June I will graduate
from High School and then go to Virginia Tech, I will
remember what Mac told me to help me go through life.
   I have enclosed a check for the Scholarship Fund, it is
a small token of my appreciation to Mac as his friendship
was priceless. If I can do anything for you please let me
Know at the below address.

                                        Respectfully

                                        Jeff Stout
                                        Jeff Stout
                                        Route 1, Box 25
                                        Stephens City, Va.
                                                 22655

Dr. Fred Collier, a Yale classmate of Mac's, sent Midge the following letter along with a personal essay (signed, "An Admiring Classmate") and some clips from the *Omaha World Herald.*

Becton Dickinson and Company
One Becton Drive
Franklin Lakes, New Jersey 07417-1880

(201) 848-6800

**BECTON
DICKINSON**

August 17, 1987

Mrs. Malcolm Baldrige
1310 33rd Street, N.W.
Washington, DC 20007

Dear Mrs. Baldrige:

This letter calls for no acknowledgement, but I wanted you to know that I, like thousands of Mac's friends, am truly devastated.

Mac and I had a friend, Gabe C. Parks, of the Omaha World Herald, with whom I grew up in Topeka. I had hoped Gabe would be able to get the entire contents of my letter to the editor printed, but as you see, it was not.

The thought was there.

Rosalie joins me in the feelings that proceed from having shared, to a small extent, the warmth which you have experienced by being exposed to such a man as your husband.

Sincerely yours,

Fred C. Collier, M.D.
Corporate Medical Director

FCC/jg
Enclosures

With the passing of H. Malcolm Baldrige, Jr., the world
lost a first-class citizen; the United States, a statesman
of superlative character whose great vision was matched by
great performance; the business community, a leader who
tempered his sound theory with the pragmatism that stems
from one who had been in the firing line; and to many
individuals, not only throughout the country, but throughout
the world, a warm, caring and thoughtful friend.

I first met Mac Baldrige in September of 1940, when we
both, scholarship students, were on our way to Yale. We
were both arriving early because of our need to find
part-time employment to help defray the cost of educational
bills which seem ridiculously small today, but in those
days, loomed of majestic proportions.

Although we both were from the middle west, Mac had
attended prep school at Hotchkiss in Lakeville, Connecticut,
and therefore, was infinitely more cosmopolitan and knowl-
edgeable about the Northeast than was I, a graduate of Topeka
High School.

Rather than showing up a green kid from Kansas to whom
Yale, at that time, was a virtually unachievable dream, Mac
Baldrige, who had a great deal of empathy and feeling for
those not as well turned out as was he, took me in tow, as
if I were a friend of long standing, shepherded me through
the mysteries of Grand Central Station, The New York, New
Haven and Hartford, the small, but incomprehensible Station

at New Haven and to the office at Yale where we both registered as Freshmen.

Although our paths diverged a few years later, when he
went with the Army to the Pacific Theatre, and I remained
behind at Yale to complete my medical studies, we kept in
touch with each other fairly frequently as members of the
tightly-knit Class of Yale, 1944.

Our Class was a fabulous one, producing governors of
two states, senators from two states, a mayor of New York
City, numerous undersecretaries in the Presidential Cabinets, justices of Courts of Appeal, and two Cabinet members,
of whom Mac served the longer term.

The Class's average was superb. Balancing off such
under-achievers as myself was Mac Baldrige, who was superior
in everything in which he was involved.

He was devoid of intellectual or professional discrimi-
nation and would answer my letters, I believe, as rapidly
and as easily as he would answer correspondence from the
Chairman of General Motors.

The last time I saw him was at a Class Dinner about two
months before his death. As guests, my wife and I had taken
old friends from Denmark, a professor of pathology and his
wife, who were here for a short visit.

How impressed they were when Mac came to our table to
speak to me in his usual gentle, humorous fashion, and what
a thrill for our guests to meet the United States Secretary

of Commerce, probably the best Secretary of Commerce the country has ever had.

As you know, Mac could write much better than this, because as a major in English at Yale, and as a communicating architect and driver of a large corporation he had to, and did, understand writing. His deftly-written and humorously-pointed memoranda from the Office of the Secretary stressed clarity in writing and avoidance of jargon and coined words.

It is difficult to write about a man who did all that he did and still wrote instructions.

We shall miss him, his personality, his accomplishments and his goals.

An Admiring Classmate

Editorial Page

Unsigned articles are the opinion of The World-Herald.

Settlement of IBP Dispute
A Chance to Move Ahead

The settlement of the 7½-month labor dispute at the IBP plant in Dakota City, Neb., was good news for the economy of northeast Nebraska and the remainder of the Sioux City area.

Some union officials have interpreted the new, four-year contract between IBP and the United Food and Commercial Workers Union Local 222 as a victory for union members. In a sense, it was. At least, the union didn't have to live with a pay cut, as it did when it went back to work in 1983 after a strike. Moreover, the union won friends this time for avoiding the kind of violence that too often in the past accompanied strikes against IBP.

On the major issues, however, IBP emerged the bigger victor. The company won a wage freeze for nearly three years. The new contract for the flagship IBP plant in Dakota City calls for a 15-cent-an-hour wage increase for workers in the last 16 months of the four-year agreement.

In an industry where give-backs have been more common than built-in annual raises, this may seem to be a victory for the union. On the other hand, that reasoning doesn't take into account the wages the meatpacking workers lost the past 7½ months. Based on a 40-hour week and 33 weeks of unemployment, a member of Local 222 who was earning $8.20 an hour as a processor lost about $10,800 in wages during the labor dispute.

What could be the biggest IBP victory was the union's acceptance of a two-tier wage structure, which allows new workers to start at pay considerably below the wages paid to union meatpackers. Because meatpacking plants have a high turnover rate, the two-tier agreement is expected to lower IBP's labor cost.

Leaders of the United Food and Commercial Workers Union wanted to get rid of the two-tier system. They had vowed to fight IBP's two-tier proposal. To have the two-tier system in the IBP contract tends to lock it in industrywide.

Jim Lyons, a union official in Sioux Falls, S.D., said, "The two-tier wage structure is just devastating to unions." Bill Buckholtz, a union official on strike at the John Morrell and Co. plant in Sioux City, said, "We're not very excited by the IBP agreement."

Officials of the union local pointed out that they achieved improved benefits in the new contract. A profit-sharing plan will be started, some work clothing will be provided, safety inspections will be expanded and the amount of medical coverage for workers will be increased.

It can be hoped that a four-year contract will result in relative harmony now between Local 222 and IBP. The packing industry is intensely competitive. That means that IBP's survival — and the health of the Midlands cattle industry — requires IBP to be efficient and highly focused.

The distraction of a strike is now behind IBP. The other energy-sapping distraction that IBP must deal with now is answering the accusation by the Occupational Safety and Health Administration that the company kept poor worker safety records. OSHA proposed a $2.6 million fine, the largest in a series of fines OSHA has proposed for what it interprets as violations of its records-keeping rules. Earlier, Chrysler Corp. and Union Carbide Corp. were accused of similar violations.

Perhaps now that the union is back in IBP's Dakota City plant, it can work in partnership with the management to meet OSHA's crackdown on record keeping and, much more important, improve actual worker safety in the plant. If IBP's accident record is worse than it should be — and no proof has been offered yet that it is — both sides of the collective-bargaining process will need to work together to improve it. Industrial safety problems are rarely the fault of only management or only the workers. True teamwork is needed to reduce accidents.

MiKE LUCKOVICH
Times-Picayune

The Public Pulse

Baldrige Remembered

Berkeley, Calif.

The shocking news of Secretary of Commerce Malcolm Baldrige's death sent my thoughts back 46 years when he and his friend, Jim Latenser, and I used to go dancing at Peony Park. Mac's presence, his ready wit and his contagious smile meant there were never awkward silences that can settle over two youngsters trying to get to know each other.

In recent years, the newspaper photographs of Baldrige have shown a sober-faced man, and no wonder. It is hard for a sensible person to keep smiling in the face of all the things that have happened since 1941. The man whom the nation now mourns bore a heavy responsibility, and it was right that he should take it seriously. But I will remember the laughing, good-natured boy who led me skillfully around the dance floor the summer before Pearl Harbor.

Virginia Foote Ireys.

'Orr Orchestration?'

Omaha.

Once again, we are treated to a curious spectacle bearing evidence of orchestration by Kay Orr

Framers Wanted Flexibility

vning farmland or engaging in agriculture unless it is a family farm corporation. To be a family farm corporation, a corporation must have the majority of its stock held by members of the same family, with at least one member actively engaged in the day-to-day labor or management of the operation.

The amendment denies, without any economic justification, unrelated people the rights that members of a family have in conducting agriculture-related business. It also has been interpreted as prohibiting commercial-scale feedlots by corporations.

To get an idea of the damaging impact of Initiative 300 on the state, one needs only review the list of agriculture-related companies that say they would have located or expanded in Nebraska if not for Initiative 300.

Some farm organization leaders who support Initiative 300 said the governor's summit meeting was unfair to the agricultural community. That's hardly the case.

State senators have, at times, been bombarded with phone calls, letters and visits from Nebraskans, including some who have no connection with agriculture, who support the amendment. It is not unfair for business leaders, some of whom depend on agriculture for their livelihood, to express their opinions on the issue.

The issue of whether the anti-corporate farming amendment is good or bad for Nebraska should not be limited to its effect on family farms. State senators also should study how the amendment is affecting the state's overall business climate.

protect themselves and society by taking the following precautions: 1) Have only one wife; 2) Have only one girlfriend; and 3) Make sure that your wife and your girlfriend are the same person.

Jon Trandt.

'A First-Class Citizen'

Franklin Lakes, N.J.

With the death of H. Malcolm Baldrige, the world has lost a first-class citizen; the United States lost a statesman of superlative character whose great vision was matched by great performance; the business community lost a leader who tempered his sound theory with the pragmatism that stems from one who had been in the firing line; and many individuals lost a warm, caring and thoughtful friend.

We shall miss him, his personality, his accomplishments and his goals.

Admiring classmate.

'Report Unsafe Truckers'

Mead, Neb.

There is something that can be done about the problem referred to by Dennis Potter Sr. (Pulse, July 25, "The Truck Hazard"). If you observe unsafe driving practices by a trucker, report him to the owner of the vehicle along with the date, time and place of the incident.

As the owner of a trucking company, I appreciate the legitimate complaints so that we can eliminate problems that our drivers may be causing. Most other companies would feel the same.

Connie Eckley.

annals of U.S. malady that, and supposedly

Now that the would be won country would government in other.

'Will Cor

Will Senato terest in Nica other liberal I cause they ren nist contras?

Congress lo make up its r the contras in back during 19 Time will right. Too bad

'The Mec

Polls indica to the contras what had been media heavil, Communist g public, have gressmen, wh

A Professor's Love of Words

John Bremner was not a headline-maker, not the way a governor or mayor is. Yet countless numbers of newspaper readers across the country have benefited from his influence on journalism.

Bremner was a purist — a word purist. Words, he said, were his professional life. Students in his university journalism classes and professional seminars were taught that spelling, grammar and proper word usage are the building blocks to good writing and editing. But Bremner went beyond the grammar books by trying to foster a love of words.

In the introduction to his book, "Words on Words," Bremner wrote: "To love anything, you must first know it. To love words, you must first know what they are. Yes, words are symbols of ideas. But many words have lives of their own. They have their own historical and etymological associations,

their own romantic and environmental dalliances, their own sonic and visual delights."

Bremner's commanding presence and flamboyant teaching style instilled that love in students at the University of Kansas, where he taught editing and writing for 16 years. He also taught at the University of Iowa and conducted seminars in classrooms and newsrooms in various parts of the nation.

The respect he earned is illustrated by the fact that several times he won the HOPE award, which is given by the K.U. student body to an outstanding educator.

John Bremner died Thursday at the age of 66. The influence of his teaching and writing, however, will continue to guide writers and editors who care about words — and that is something readers can appreciate.

'Few Right Fielders in Soviet Union'

Well, Not Even Earl'

Washington.

I see by the papers, as Will Rogers used to say, that the Soviet Union has taken up the great game of baseball.

Bill Keller of The New York Times, reporting from Moscow, says the Russians not only are playing baseball; they also are claiming they invented baseball. Fifteen teams have been organized. A baseball commissar, Alexandr Kalivod, has been named. Before long, it is alleged, the Tashkent Subway Builders may be ready for international play.

Somehow it all seems a little unlikely. Unreliable sources tell me that Earl Weaver, onetime boss of the Baltimore Orioles, this summer took on a consulting job for the Tallinn Tractors. Reportedly he found the going tough.

At the first team meeting, Weaver attempted to discuss balls and strikes with his prospective players. If a hitter got four balls, he explained, the hitter was entitled to take a walk.

"Nyet!" cried Mikhail Mikhailovitch, a candidate for shortstop. "In the Soviet Union, is no balls. Is trappings of czarist decadence. Here we have folk dance only, or sometime is ballet. We make it four ballets, hokay?"

Weaver undertook to define the strike zone. Weaver has been undertaking to define the strike zone for American umpires for 50 years without notable success. He fared no better in Estonia.

"Strikes?" cried Andrei Andreiovitch, a potential outfielder. "In Soviet Union we have no strikes. In this land of freedom, no one free to strike. Even one strike and you're out — way out! Three strikes? You talk impossible stuff."

Weaver was not discouraged. Suppose, he supposed, we get a man on first base. His pupils seemed to grasp the idea. And suppose, Weaver

further supp weak arm and windup. Da, d Weaver, we s the base!

This propo Gregor Greg catches, som plained that s incompatible Soviet Union.

"Here we h "In Commun in common. base!"

Weaver sa steal his own base.

"Why, the Murmurs of ; question. "Or the Soviet wa Weaver ha going at all w the team's di see that the been bushhog

Furthermore...

Alfred Pattavina will return to a familiar office when he takes over as Omaha public safety director Monday. Pattavina, who has worked as a police officer and also served as public safety director for Mayors Eugene Leahy and Edward Zorinsky, should be able to continue the process of healing the rifts that developed between City Hall and the police department during the administration of Michael Boyle. Mayor Simon made a wise choice by hiring Pattavina.

Today's regular monthly test of Omaha's civil defense siren system won't be as routine as others have over the years. In two tests in July, the system didn't work properly, prompting

concern that some parts of the city might not be adequately warned in the event of a tornado. City officials say the damaged sirens have been repaired — each of the 50 sirens is expected to sound off during the 10 a.m. test. That would provide a degree of welcome reassurance to Omahans.

A case of delusion? Officials of the National Education Association expressed disappointment that some Republican Party officials were cool to the pitch for greater GOP support of the association's work. How could they realistically expect any other reaction? The association routinely endorses Democratic candidates in state and national elections.

Mac Baldrige, Straight Shooter

He was born in the Midlands. His value system was formed in his early years in Omaha public schools and on a ranch in western Nebraska.

When he died, he was eulogized by Lou Cannon, White House correspondent for the Washington Post, as a "straight shooter." The Old West phrase fit Commerce Secretary Howard Malcolm Baldrige perfectly.

His interest in the West, in riding and in calf roping, never left him, not through the years at Hotchkiss Preparatory School, not at Yale nor his service as chief executive officer of a multimillion-dollar corporation that he rescued from the edge of failure in 1962.

At age 64, Baldrige was still competing in professional rodeos. He was practicing at a California ranch last weekend when his horse inexplicably reared and fell on him, fatally injuring him.

The son of an Omaha attorney who served in the Nebraska Legislature, on the MUD board and for one term in the House of Representatives from the 2nd District, Baldrige attended the old Columbian Elementary School and Central High School before going to prep school in Connecticut. His mother and father lived in Omaha until 1945.

Baldrige was one of three original members of President Reagan's Cabinet. His reputation, even among Reagan opponents, was untarnished by even so much as a hint of scandal. He was a consistent advocate of free trade, helping to formulate the president's trade policies.

"Free trade is absolutely necessary to the future economic well-being of the world," Baldrige said. Free trade, however, must be tempered by an insistence on fair trade because "our fair trade laws are the bedrock on which free trade stands."

Baldrige pushed early in Reagan's first term for stronger trade measures, but it wasn't until Reagan's second term that the administration took a tougher line. In April, Reagan imposed 100 percent duties on some Japanese products after the Japanese were found to have sold computer chips on the U.S. market at less than cost.

Baldrige's death came as Congress was getting ready to select a conference committee to fashion a trade bill from House and Senate measures that require strong retaliation against foreign traders. Reagan has threatened to veto such a bill because he said it would start a trade war, a view influenced by Baldrige. Baldrige's influence on the trade bill conferees will be missed.

As his longtime friend, Vice President George Bush, said: "Mac Baldrige set the standard for excellence, decency and integrity in public life. He was a tower of strength and truly a man of honor."

—*Omaha World Herald*